The
Job Search Cookbook

A Recipe for Strategic Job Search Management

John-Paul Hatala, Ph.D.

GET IN THE FLOW
PUBLISHING

The Job Search Cookbook
Copyright 2012 © John-Paul Hatala

Book design by Clark Kenyon

ISBN – 0-9821286-0-6
ISBN – 978-0-9821286-0-2

The publisher offers special discounts on bulk orders of this book.
For more information, please contact:

Manager of Special Sales
Get in the Flow Publishing
1-877-356-9675

PRINTED IN THE UNITED STATES OF AMERICA

10 9 8 7 6 5 4 3 2 1

FIRST EDITION

DEDICATION

TO MY MOTHER WHO CONTINUTES TO SUPPORT ME IN ALL MY ENDEAVORS.

Introduction

Has someone ever told you that looking for work is a full-time job? What does it truly mean when we say looking for work is a full-time job? You've probably heard this from someone who is already working. Some might say that it's looking for work every moment of your day, while others would say it means putting aside a couple of hours a day to work on looking for a job. In my experience working with job seekers, I've had lengthy discussions on this topic. I believe it is important that those individuals who are looking for work establish their own answer to this important question. Structuring your job search will be the *key* to your success. Let me repeat that... Structuring your job search is the *key* to your success.

Without structure, you will start to experience a downturn in your job search activity.

When we are working we are automatically provided with some structure. We have a start time and an end time. When we wake up in the morning we know that we have to show up somewhere to begin our daily routine. At the end of the day we know when we can go home. With these start and stop times we are able to work within established parameters, which provide the structure necessary to plan our lives accordingly. When looking for work, there is no one making sure that you're starting at a specific time and ending when you should. It's entirely up to you. After all, you're the boss and what you do during your search is entirely your responsibility.

Although this can be empowering and uplifting, it can be discouraging at the same time if we don't have a clear direction or haven't applied a specific structure to our job search. So when you think of your search in these terms you can relate the entire process to being self-employed, then it follows that you're waiting for your first sale...the sale of course being the job you're going to get. This book and the processes included will provide you with the structure necessary to effectively conduct your job search. Without structure, you will start to experience a downturn in your job search activity (see Job Search Forces), which will inevitably delay the time it takes you to find work. The purpose of this book is to provide structure so that you can confidently and more importantly, patiently conduct your job search. The reality is that it takes time to find work and if you're in sync with what you need to do, you will be better prepared and more motivated in continuing with your job search.

This book will guide you in the direction of becoming employed or moving up within your profession. The key word here is **guide**. My experience from working with clients who are seeking employment has taught me to focus on facilitating the process. To be honest, no one will ever truly know the trials and tribulations you have to deal with or experience during your job search. My approach has always been to assist people by guiding them in answering their own questions, respecting their goal of becoming employed. The purpose of this book is to provide a framework that will assist you as you make the journey through the various challenges in finding work.

This book will walk you through an entirely new concept regarding conducting a job search. In addition to this new concept, you will have the opportunity to manage your job search by accessing an online job search management system (you can create a free account at www.snagpad.com) or simply using a computer spreadsheet. Later in the book, you will be introduced to the Job Search Board and how you can use this tool to reduce the time it takes to find employment. Whatever method you choose, it is important to know exactly what you are doing during the Job Search Process in order to determine what is working well and what needs improvement. Whether working alone or with a job coach, the goal of a successful job search is the ability to generate job leads. The Job Search Board will assist you in determining the type of contacts you are making and how you are utilizing your job opportunities.

Undoubtedly, you have received a fair amount of advice from individuals with whom you are in contact regarding finding a job. At times it must feel like you are being bombarded with all kinds of information. This book has been structured to provide information only when you have reached a certain stage of willingness in the Job Search Process. It will walk you through the Job Search Process and help you to identify what assistance you may need, and when you need it. Working with job seekers has taught me that if individuals are going to benefit from the information I provide them, they have to be ready to receive it.

TABLE OF CONTENTS

PREFACE: A JOB SEARCH MANAGEMENT RECIPE

What's Cooking got to do with Finding a Job?

When you think of a cookbook, you most likely picture step-by-step instructions for making a number of different dishes. Each of the recipes include a list of ingredients, the utensils required to make the dish, and the amount of time it will take to complete it. Now imagine trying to make a dish without any instructions or directions. Where do you start? Most likely you would take a wild guess as to what would go into it and how to go about it, but in the end you probably would not have produced a dish that tasted as it was supposed to. So basically, the recipe provides the precise instructions necessary to make a dish turn out the way it was intended to be. Sometimes, although a dish doesn't turn out the way it was supposed to, it is true you'd likely eventually get the hang of it with practice and repeated attempts, and produce something that everyone could enjoy.

If you think about your job search in the same way as cooking a meal, you'll save a lot of time finding a job and the frustration that goes along with it. Like preparing a great dish, a job search involves a number of steps required for successfully finding a job. This book has been written to provide you with easy-to-follow instructions to finding employment, as quickly as possible. By following this job search "recipe", you will uncover a systematic process for working your way through your job search, in an organized and timely manner. Like any good recipe, the cook is the critical component to the success of a great dish. Not unlike cooking, the job seekers' goal is to follow a recipe that allows them to identify what's required and work on issues that are causing challenges in finding a job. If you are willing to follow this job search recipe, you will not only find a job, but also decrease the time it takes to get there.

There have been several books written on job search techniques. They tend to cover the full gamut of various approaches to looking for work. This book will highlight several key ingredients of the job search, with one of them focused on the way we manage the job search process. Unlike other self-help job search books, I have attempted to organize this book in such a way that resembles one of your favourite recipes. **A recipe includes the required ingredients and provides directions for making the dish.** I'm not trying to reinvent the wheel; I simply want to provide everyone with a recipe that will help them navigate through the job search process, as quickly and easily as possible. You will find the book divided into 4 parts: a job search recipe; the job search ingredients; a step-by-step method for implementing the job search ingredients; concluding with "let it stand for five minutes and serve". Each section deals with specific components of how you can manage your job search process.

I have found over the years that most people I work with are very visual. The more visual I have made my counselling sessions, the easier it has been for clients to grasp what it was I was trying to tell them and, in turn, the more successful they have been in finding a job. By the end of this book you will have been presented with a visual representation of the job search process along with effective techniques for overcoming obstacles, as you search for that perfect job.

How to Use the Job Search Cookbook

The job search cookbook has been developed as an interactive approach to the job search process. I highly recommend that you read the book from start to finish, the first time. There are some job search concepts presented here that require familiarization, in order to get the most out of this unique approach to looking for work. After you have read through the book once, you most likely will refer to more specific parts of the book as you conduct your job search.

Throughout the cookbook you will come across a number of job search aides. These include:

- **Job Search Snack (JSS)**

- **Job Search Activity (JSA)**

- **Taste Test (TT)**

These aides have been scattered throughout the cookbook in order to provide you with job search tips, exercises, and knowledge retention activities.

What is the Job Search Management Recipe?

The Job Search Management Recipe involves a process that will help guide you through the trials and tribulations of looking for work. What makes this approach unique is that it will allow you to closely monitor your progress and help you to isolate specific behaviours affecting your ability to find a job. The system involves a unique approach to looking for work by taking into account the job seeker and ensuring that he/she has some sense of control throughout the job search process. Through the use of a job search board, you will learn to effectively manage each job opportunity throughout the job search process. Believe it or not, there are stages to following a job opportunity through to being hired, and if you're not moving through each stage in a timely manner, your likelihood for getting the job is dramatically reduced. The Job Search Recipe will allow you to stay on top of your opportunities, and assist you in either working on your own or with a job search coach.

This book will walk you through the various intricacies of the Job Search Recipe and introduce you to concepts that, at first, may seem counter intuitive. Keep in mind that this recipe is proven and can help you decrease the time it takes to find employment. Like anything new, you must open yourself up to trying some things that go against what you would normally think. The key to finding the job *you* want is being able to differentiate yourself from hundreds of other candidates. This system will allow you to separate yourself from competing job hunters and help you move to the head of the line. As well, this book will compliment the job search skills you already possess, and encourage you to approach things in an entirely different way.

Who Can Use this Book?

Anyone that is presently looking for employment or is in the process of helping someone to look for work can benefit from using the techniques included in this job search book. Whether you're a job seeker, career counsellor or job search coach, this book will provide a recipe that can decrease the time it takes to find employment. As the author, my goal is to provide you with a framework for making the transition back into the labour market or for those individuals considering changing jobs. A step-by-step methodology will be presented, as well as techniques for conducting a successful job search.

What's in the Job Search Cookbook?

Differentiate yourself from hundreds of other candidates.

I have been working with individuals seeking employment for the last decade or so. I have worked with youth, welfare recipients, employment insurance recipients, professionals, and friends. It has always been my approach to deal with clients on an individual basis. The goal of this book has been to make this work applicable to all. We all have our own approach to finding employment. Our resumes, cover letters and interview skills are unique to our backgrounds and experience. Rather than write a book that was specific to one section of the population, my intention was to develop a framework that would compliment everyone's existing job search approach, and assist them towards employment. **After all, the most successful approach to looking for employment is the approach that lands the job.** The individuals who I have worked with that have been the most successful have been those individuals who have been able to understand the job search process, and not just for the short-term. Job searching is something that will occur throughout our lives. Statistics tell us that each of us will go through six or seven career changes. Who knows how many jobs we'll have! Understanding the job search process allows us to identify strategies that enable us to move smoothly through the hiring process. If we can isolate the problematic issues we are experiencing, we may avoid being caught in a never ending spiral of unemployment or, even worse, end up with a job with which we are not totally satisfied.

Before you get started, I would like to address the notion of career and employment counselling. If you are reading this book I assume that you are presently looking for a job or are ready to commence with

your job search; you have put your resume and cover letter together, practiced your interview skills, identified what direction you are going to pursue, in terms of the type of employment you are looking for, and discovered what your skills, abilities and interests are. If you haven't, I highly recommend utilizing a professional career or employment counsellor. These professionals will take the time to explore with you the different options and interests you have, and assist you in identifying a career direction. If you are unable to meet with a counsellor, there are many online resources that will enable you to identify some of the options you have. In the course of assisting individuals in finding employment over the years, I have preferred to call myself an employment facilitator versus an employment counsellor for the simple reason that whenever I was working with individuals, I was facilitating the job search process rather than counselling them. If issues of a personal nature came up that I could see affected the individual's ability to find a job, which many times they did, I would simply refer them to a professional who was trained in dealing with those specific issues. I always felt that if I presented myself as a facilitator, I could train my clients to become their own facilitator and learn the skills necessary in looking for employment for the rest of their lives.

So, you have been working on identifying the type of job you would like: something that matches your skills and background, and -- don't forget -- it has to be something that you would like to do for 40 hours a week. You have your materials in hand: several copies of your resume and cover letter. You have been working diligently on your interview skills and you're ready to look for that perfect job. The first part of the job search is complete! Now what?

The first part is the secure stage. You get to dream about that job you have always wanted. You discover yourself. You now know what you like and what you dislike. The only bad part of stage one is that you eventually have to move on to stage two, which is to look for that perfect job. You have to go out and identify some of the opportunities that are a match for your job goals. You have to send out resumes by fax, email or regular mail, or actually go out to some of these companies and fill out applications and submit resumes. Then, you get to go home and wait by the phone for one of these companies to call you and offer you an interview. Sometimes, you get lucky and you get a call right away. However, the rest of the time you never hear back, even though you've taken the time to fill out an application or submit a resume. How dare they! Do they not know how long it has taken you to prepare for this moment? Do they not know that you have the right skills, experience and determination for this job, and are a better candidate than anyone else? It just doesn't seem fair. Remember, identifying your skills and interests, putting your resume and cover letter together and submitting them to a handful of companies is the easiest part. Accepting the fact that you are gong to experience rejection like you have never felt before, and managing the job search process is the hard part, and it is key to your job searching success. If you are unable to deal with this, your ability to conduct an effective job search may be compromised.

Remember: knowing how to effectively job search is something that will continue to be relevant throughout all of our lives. There are few jobs out there that you will be able to keep until you retire. Job changes occur on a regular basis, and for that very reason we need to understand the dynamics of searching for new employment, and all the intricacies involved.

Job Search Snack: (JSS: P-1) Career Development Online Resources

National Career Development Association	http://www.ncda.org
Contact Point	http://www.contactpoint.ca
Occupational Outlook Handbook	http://www.doleta.gov/
National Association of Colleges and Employers	http://www.naceweb.org/
Canadian Association of Colleges and Employers	http://www.cacee.com
Service Canada Employment Services	http://www.servicecanada.gc.ca/eng/ subjects/employment/index.shtml
U.S. Department of Labor	http://www.dol.gov
America's Career Info Net	http://www.acinet.org/

Part One: Setting the Stage

I've never had a client who said looking for employment was fun; it's not, it's hard work. Job hunters particularly face a lot of rejection and uncertainty alongside daily personal and financial pressures, just

to name a few. The need to manage the Job Search Process becomes that much more important in maintaining your motivation and sanity in order to realistically continue the pursuit of employment. For example, when it comes to looking for a job, the more realistic you are about an opportunity, the better prepared you will be to deal with potential rejection. Throughout my career I have been challenged in dealing with individuals who need a job, but lose their motivation to continue looking for one. Being realistic means you are not going to get every job that you apply for. In fact, your will be hearing far more "no's" than "yes's". To tell you otherwise would – I hate to say it - be very unrealistic. But if you begin to understand that there is a *process* to looking for employment, then it makes sense that the more you understand this process, the more likely you are to be realistic about your chances, and the better able you'll be to maintain your motivation. Not only will your motivational level be maintained, but your ability to identify certain issues that are problematic in finding employment will become more apparent, allowing you to correct them for when you are chasing down future opportunities, and ultimately increase your chances for success. Part One will walk you through the Job Search Forces you will be encountering and provide ways to deal with them

Part Two: Gathering the Ingredients

Job Search Snack: (JSS: P-2) Job Search Forces

1. Activity

2. Motivation

3. Reality

The Job Search Management Recipe includes five (5) ingredients and focuses on those individuals who are ready to look for employment. Part Two of the book will go through the specific elements that make up the Job Search Ingredients in detail. The first ingredient is the ability of an individual to understand their ***job search numbers***. Here, we will explore the importance of maintaining the level of activity necessary for increasing your chances for employment. The second ingredient provides methods for monitoring ***what you do*** during your job search. Understanding what you would normally do will assist you in identifying ways to deal with any specific issues that may be impeding your chances for employment success. Most importantly, if you are working with a job search coach, your ability to communicate what you are doing during your job search will allow them to more effectively help you. The third ingredient looks specifically at the ***Hiring Cycle*** and the importance of understanding timing as a factor in determining whether or not you have a greater chance of securing employment. Surveys have revealed that there is a timeframe to every company's Hiring Cycle and that if you are not moving within that Hiring Cycle, your chances for employment are drastically reduced. The fourth ingredient looks at one's ability to generate ***the next step*** at various points throughout the Hiring Cycle. This component will provide methods for moving through the Job Search Process in a direction that increases your likelihood for employment.

The final ingredient will provide you with a way to monitor your ***Job Search Process*** and ways for managing each step. Understanding the Job Search Process is critical to your success. Attaching a timeframe to this process ensures that you are on top of each job opportunity in order to maximize your chances for employment success.

Job Search Snack: (JSS: P-3) Job Search Recipe Ingredients

1. Job Search Numbers

2. The What, Who, When, Where and Why

3. The Hiring Cycle

4. The Next Step

5. The Job Search Process

Part Three: Walking through the Job Search Process

In addition to the five key ingredients in the Job Search Recipe, Part Three will take you through the Job Search Process one step at a time and highlight strategies for moving through the job search stages in a timely manner. You have the ingredients and now it's time to put them all together and start cooking. This section will provide you with the job search utensils and will show you specific ways to manage your job search opportunities, and ways for identifying whether these job leads are worth hanging onto.

Part Four: Implementing the job search cookbook strategies

Part Four will provide some tips and identify some of the challenges associated with moving through the Job Search Process. More specifically, Part Four represents the beginning of your job search renewal. When someone tells you that looking for work is a full-time job, you'll be able to tell them exactly what this means.

Job Search Activity: (JSA: P-1) On the lines listed below, list your present or planned job search activities (examples of activities are provided).

1. *Make cold calls between 2:00 and 4:00* _____

2. *Research my industry of interest, regarding hiring trends* _____

3. _____

4. _____

5. _____

6. _____

7. _____

8. _____

9. _____

10. _____

11. _____

12. _____

Job Search Snack: (JSS: P-4) Job Search Recipe Ingredients

1. Targeted resume (See example JSS: 2-6)

2. Generic resume (See example JSS: 2-7)

3. Cover letter template (See example JSS: 2-8)

4. Action Plans A & B (See example JSS: 1-2)

5. Job Search Board

COMMON TERMS IN THE JOB SEARCH PROCESS

Application: This requires a job seeker to visit the job opportunity to fill out an employer-specific form. In most cases the application is accompanied by a resume.

Continuous Job Search: The continuous job search is something that happens after the individual finds a job. Once employment has been secured, the individual then has access to resources that were previously not available (i.e. new contacts). By maintaining momentum once employed, the individual can achieve his or her ultimate career goals by continuing to identify job opportunities through the Job Search Process.

Generic Resume: This is a resume that is delivered to all job leads and is not specifically customized to suit a particular position or employer.

Hiring Cycle: This is defined as the time an employer posts an available position until they fill it. The Job Search Process is associated with a Hiring Cycle, and if an individual is not moving from step to step within that cycle, the likelihood for employment success is drastically reduced.

Job Card: Job cards are created on www.snagpad.com, which is an online job search board management system. Job opportunities are converted into job cards so that a user can automatically manage their job search via the Internet.

Job Lead: A job lead represents a job opening. However, a lead can also be that which directs a job seeker to a specific individual within an organization (i.e., supervisor).

Job Opportunity: A Job Opportunity is a potential job lead. It can be identified via the newspaper, an Internet job board, an employment center, a head hunter, an employment agency, a friend, family, an acquaintance, an employment counsellor or a complete stranger.

Job Related-Information: is information that may lead to a job opportunity. The result could be an actual job, a referral to an employer, or labour market information.

Job Search Board: This is a tool that assists job seekers in monitoring their Job Search Process. The Job Search Board has six columns: Opportunity, Applied, Set Interview, Interview, Job Offer and Job. Each column represents a unique stage regarding an individual's job search efforts and allows one to monitor one's progress each step of the way. The Job Search Board is available in a folder format or by going online to www.snagpad.com. The reader can sign up for a 'free' account and refer to the Job Search Board to visualize the Job Search Process, as they go through this book (See 'What's Next').

Job Search Coach: is an individual who assists people that are ready to commence with their job search. This means that the job seeker has developed an Action Plan and knows the type of work they are specifically looking for.

Job Search Counsellor: is an individual who works with people throughout the entire process, including conducting: a needs assessment, career exploration and job search activities.

Job A: Job A is an employment goal that is highly desirable and matches the individual's skills, abilities and experience. When putting together an Action Plan, Job A represents the desired job and is not necessarily based on a realistic attempt to secure employment in the designated area.

Job B: Job B compliments Job A in that it is a secondary goal for finding employment. Job B involves identifying job opportunities that temporarily replace a Job A. Job B should focus on employment opportunities that help make the individual more competitive for their job A. Job B does not necessarily have to focus on the job itself, but more specifically on the organization wherein the opportunity for growth is possible.

Job Search Process: The Job Search Process refers to the various stages of a job search. This includes everything from identifying the job opportunity to starting the job.

Job Search Snacks: While you read the book, these little "nibbles" are essential job search tips that are both quick and easy to read, and highlight key points made throughout the book.

Next Step: A Next Step refers to moving from stage to stage within the Job Search Process.

Opportunity-Card: This card is where a single job opportunity or lead is recorded in the Job Search Board. The information should various columns, including: company name, position, job description, next steps, application date, interview date, contact name, contact phone, contact email, contact fax number.

Recipe: This contains step-by-step directions to finding a job.

Social Network: is a group of individuals that are either connected directly or indirectly with each other, and are providers (i.e. sources) of information that may lead an individual towards his or her goal.

Social Networking: is the act of developing contacts and gathering information that will assist in the completion of a goal or objective. Social networking skills include: building rapport, critical thinking, organizational skills, verbal and oral skills development, and negotiation skills.

Social Network Audit: is a process for examining one's social network. The goal of the audit is to determine the types of contacts that exist, and how they may potentially be of assistance in finding employment. The social network audit is about identifying what the contacts in one's social network know and how this information can help a job seeker find a job.

SnagPad.com: Snagpad.com is an online tool that allows job seekers to virtually manage their job search via the Internet. Accounts can be set up at http://www.snagpad.com.

Targeted Resume: is a customized resume intended for a specific position or employer. No two targeted resumes are the same.

Taste Test: A Taste Test provides an opportunity for you to test your knowledge on certain sections of the book. When you come to a Taste Test, complete the test and find the answers in the appendices.

PART ONE

PART ONE: THE PREPARATION, BEFORE YOU START TO COOK

Before you Start to Cook

Like any great recipe, there is some preparation required before you get to slide the dish into the oven. The same holds true for effectively managing a job search. The Job Search Recipe presented in this book has some fundamental underpinnings that should be considered, before commencing with your job search. The areas that we will initially cover include the following:

- Putting a Job Search Plan together
- Sharing control in the Job Search Process
- Understanding the Job Search Forces

In my experience working with a number of job seekers, the number one cause of failure was their inability to remain *motivated* throughout their job search. If you're already employed, you may not feel the same forces at play as someone unemployed, regarding motivation. However, I have also worked with individuals that were desperate to get out of their present employment position and required a level of motivation to continue. The biggest factor that you need to remember in looking for work is that it takes time to find a job. If you find a job in the first couple of weeks, you're one of the lucky ones. The process may take weeks for one single job opportunity. Because of this, you must be able to maintain a level of commitment for a period of time that may be beyond what you expect. That's why it's important to deal with some issues up front, prior to getting into the specific techniques to the job search. If you don't anticipate such issues upfront, it's going to adversely affect your job search. That is why I have dedicated the first part of the book to dealing with the psychological as well as technical aspects of the process. In some cases you may consider speaking with a job search coach or career counsellor to discuss how these areas may affect you. I've found over the years that if my clients understand the factors affecting a job search prior to starting, success rates dramatically increase.

1. Identifying your Job A and Job B

As was mentioned in the introduction, this book is useful if you have identified the type of career or job you are trying to obtain. A number of things must be considered, but most importantly a Job Search Plan must be developed. In most cases, job seekers like to only focus on one type of job they are interested in acquiring. However, I like to encourage all my clients to come up with an alternate type of job that could make them more competitive for the job they truly want, just in case the first one is deemed to be not viable at the moment.

Understanding the job search process allows us to identify strategies that enable us to move smoothly through the hiring process.

The one thing that you cannot control in the Job Search Process is the labour market conditions. For example, you may have all the necessary skills and experience to find a job as a computer programmer, but the market might not require that type of job at the time you're looking for work, in spite of your background. The question then becomes, what can I do in the meantime until the market conditions change and there is a demand for programmers again. This is where a Job B comes in to play. Job B involves an alternative plan that gets you to your Job A. Let's take the example of a computer programmer. Although there are a number of variations of computer programmer positions, for this example we'll keep it fairly generic. If you're looking for work as a computer programmer, but the labour market indicates low demand, you have to decide on something that will ultimately lead you to getting the job you want at a point later in the future. As was mentioned previously, looking for work, technically, never ends, so if you're able to be successful with Job B, you will continue to try and acquire Job A.

With regards to seeking a computer programmer position, it may be possible to get another position that may not necessarily deal specifically with computer programming, but is somewhat linked. For example, you may consider trying to get into an IT department to do something else (e.g. technician). By taking a job that is not specific to Job A, but is linked through Job B, you have a couple of options. The first option would be to wait until something becomes available in your specific field. This, of course, is assuming that the organization that you start to work with has the potential to expand, or some of the existing employees are close to retirement. Indeed, these are considerations that one needs to be aware of as he or she conducts a job search. However, the second option is to take a position that does not fall directly within your speciality, but is within your area of interest nonetheless; the idea here is that this would suffice as employment as you continue your job search. By doing this, a potential employer won't see any gaps in your resume, nor will they see that you have been outside your area of interest. However, there is a third option wherein you focus on the organization and not the position. Once you have found a job (the job doesn't really matter) with a company that provides *potential for growth*, you can work towards climbing the ladder. Also, by working within an organization that has growth potential, you will have access to resources otherwise not available to you. When you've resorted to your Job B, your search for an organization should include these characteristics:

- *What is the opportunity for advancement?*

- *How does the company view professional development?*

- *Are there are number of locations throughout the city, state, country?*

- *Do they have an employee development plan?*

- *Do the have a leadership program?*

- *Is there formal succession planning?*

- *Is there an organizational culture that fosters promotion from within the organization?*

- *Is the organization unionized and, if so, how does that impact advancement?*

- *How often are performance reviews conducted and are they linked to salary*

- *Increases/promotions?*

- *What is the organizational chart look like? Is it fairly flat (i.e. few management positions) or*

- *Diverse (i.e. many management positions)?*

The next thing you should do is set up some criteria for your Job B job. Following the example of a computer programmer, what skills and experiences should you obtain in order to increase your value for Job A? You probably should gain access to specific experiences or acquire new

skills. Whatever the reason, you need to link the Job B job to your Job A so that when you do get an interview for a "Job A" you have created value for yourself in the eyes of the employer, through your "Job B" experiences.

Parallel Job Search

Most individuals conduct a job search by looking for only their Job A. As time goes by and these seekers are unsuccessful in finding a job, they start to lower their expectations and look for other types of work. This is problem with this is that they have wasted time focusing on one type of job, which obviously has limited the number of opportunities. The unfortunate reality is that our Job A's may take time to find. We have to be realistic in the face of our chances. So instead of waiting to look at Job B's, why not run a parallel job search and look for both types of jobs *from the beginning*. This will save you a lot of time and open you up to a greater amount of job possibilities, right from the get-go. As long as you have established some criteria for why you would take a Job B, you then possess a sound rationale for having moved in that direction when you finally get your Job A.

Job Search Snack: (JSS: 1-1) Sample Job Search Plan for Job A & B

Job A & B: The Action Plan is two-fold: 1) Job A; and 2) Job B. Job A deals with your ideal job and closely matches your skills, abilities, salary expectations, location, etc. Job B highlights an alternative job that you are willing to take in order to help you reach your primary job goal. When identifying your secondary job goal, the organization is more important than the actual job. You should be looking for opportunity for growth within the organization and the addition of new contacts to your network. Networking through job contacts is a great opportunity for new job leads, promotion and career change.

DATE OF ACTION PLAN: *September 16, 2012*
ACTION PLAN TIME FRAME: *12 weeks*
PERSONAL GOAL(S): *My main personal goal is to develop and improve my time management skills.*
PLAN FOR ACHIEVING PERSONAL GOAL: *I plan on taking a workshop at my local employment resource center. In addition, I will be working with a job search coach to assist me in the Job Search Process.*
JOB A: *TO FIND A POSITION AS A RESTAURANT MANAGER*

Industry: *Hospitality*

Job Title: *Manager*

Job Responsibilities: *payroll, scheduling, operations, human resource management*

Skills Required: *leadership, strategic thinking, budgeting, organization, strong communication ability*

Experience Required: *2-3 years in management*

Education Required: *college diploma*

Average Hiring Cycle for Industry: *3 weeks, 5-6 weeks for management*

Gaps in Resume for Job: *lack of experience in a management position*

JOB B (CRITERIA): *TO FIND AN ASSISTANT MANAGER POSITION IN THE HOSPITALITY INDUSTRY*

Criteria for Taking a "Job B"

- Leadership opportunities
- Strategizing
- Working with budgets
- Practice communication skills
- Exposure to HR practices
- Hiring staff
- Making contacts

Links to job goal A: *working as an assistant to a manager, which provides access to other opportunities within the organization and builds on my experience.*

Industry: *Hospitality*

Job Title: Assistant Manager

Job Responsibilities: *Assists the manager*

Skills Required: *leadership, communication skills, strategic planning, critical thinking*

Experience Required: *work in a restaurant*
Education Required: *High School Diploma*
Average Hiring Cycle for Industry: *3-4 weeks*
Gaps in Resume to Job: *none*
EXPECTED LENGTH OF JOB SEARCH: *8 weeks, as per industry hiring standards*
HOW GAPS IN RESUME WILL BE FILLED: *will work on lack of experience, by volunteering and networking*
RESUME(S) TO BE CREATED: *generic resume and customized resume, based on each job opportunity*
COVER LETTER(S) TO BE CREATED: *a generic cover letter with opening paragraph geared toward specific job opportunity*
TECHNIQUES TO BE USED FOR IDENTIFYING JOB LEADS: *Networking, job ads, Internet, cold calling*
INDIVIDUALS INVOLVED IN MY JOB SEARCH: *Friends, family, teachers, and all of their contacts*

Job Search Activity: *(JSA: 1-1) Creating a Job Search Plan for Job A & B*

Fill in the following chart with as much detail as possible. Remember that this is essential to getting the Job Search Recipe just right. If you require assistance in filling this out, work with a career or employment counselor.

DATE OF ACTION PLAN:
ACTION PLAN TIME FRAME:
PERSONAL GOAL(S):
JOB A: Industry: Job Title: Job Responsibilities: Skills Required: Experience Required: Education Required: Average Hiring Cycle for Industry: Gaps in Resume to Obtaining Job:
JOB B: Criteria (Reasons) for taking a Job B •

-
-
-
-

Links to job goal A:

Industry:

Job Title:

Job Responsibilities:

Skills Required:

Experience Required:

Education Required:

Average Hiring Cycle for Industry:

Gaps in Resume to Job:

EXPECTED LENGTH OF JOB SEARCH:

HOW GAPS IN RESUME WILL BE FILLED:

RESUME(S) TO BE CREATED:

COVER LETTER(S) TO BE CREATED:

TECHNIQUES TO BE USED FOR IDENTIFYING JOB LEADS:

INDIVIDUALS INVOLVED IN MY JOB SEARCH:

2. Sharing Control in the Job Search Process

One of the biggest challenges in finding a job is being able to maintain your motivation or, at least, some kind of momentum. The problem with this concept is that most of us feel that, as job searchers, we have no control in the face of an employment opportunity. "How can I feel in control if the employer is the one who makes the decision on the individual they select for the position?" This was the common question I would hear from my clients whenever we would speak about control and the job searching process. The reality is that employers do have a lot of control. They're the ones who make the decision as to who to hire. There are a number of different reasons an employer might choose one candidate over another. Whether it's an entry level position within a large corporation or a gas station clerk, decisions are made based on an employer's perception of how a person would fit into their organization and whether or not they can contribute. However, sometimes, it's not as complex as that. Perhaps the employer doesn't actually know what they want, either because they were never properly trained in effective hiring procedures or simply because they were simply thrown into the task of hiring someone. As job searchers, we may never know what the answer is. However, it's our job to find out as much information as possible nonetheless, so that we can make decisions to move the Job Search Process forward. Also, you must keep in mind that you are in the process of conducting a job search. This means that you are considering your available options regarding employment. So if an employer asks during an interview how much money are you looking for, your response should sound something like this: "As you're probably aware, I'm in the process of conducting a job search and I've discovered that the range of salary has been anywhere from X to Y. Where would you say you fall within this range for this position?" Notice how I did not refer to industry ranges, but focused the employer on what I was experiencing through my job search. This gives you credibility as well as helping you deal with an awkward question. More importantly, it demonstrates to the employer that you're conducting a job search, you're knowledgeable about the competition and that you have some control. Telling the employer you're in the process of conducting a job search basically says that if they think you're the right candidate, they'd better hurry, otherwise you're going to go somewhere else. This is a critical point and something job seekers often overlook.

> *Job Search Snack:* **(JSS: 1-2) Remember that you're conducting a job search**
>
> *Always remind employers, and anyone you know, that you're in the process of conducting a job search.* This will allow you to present yourself in such a way as to appear as though you are considering your options and will allow you to feel more control in the Job Search Process. When an employer knows you're conducting a job search, a sense of urgency is created as they may think you might go somewhere else.

Let's turn the tables around for a moment. What if the job searcher was in total control? What if there was such a huge demand for workers that you could choose exactly where you wanted to work? What would you look for in an employer? Would it be the pay, job quality, the environment, or even the type of boss you would be reporting to? You can see how, in this scenario, the control dynamic has shifted. Now that you're in control, you can choose for

whom you want to work and under what conditions. As you look at this example, ask yourself: Why couldn't it always be this way? After all, you *are* in the middle of a job search. Moreover, you're not going to apply to only one job.

Of course, it is not always possible to be in control of the Job Search Process. The employer is the one who decides when they require new employers. They ultimately choose the candidate. Given that, it might sound a bit odd that you could potentially have control of the Job Search Process. I've worked with clients who were on the brink of quitting their job search because of the lack of control they felt they were experiencing. They would come back to my office after an interview and tell me that they "nailed it" and that there was no way the employer would pass them up, only to learn a few days later that they were not selected for the position. In that situation there is absolutely no control on the job seeker's side. But what if you weren't looking for *total* control? What if you wanted to share control and, at the same time, become more proactive in the Job Search Process? In Part 2 of this book, we'll go into more detail on this topic, but before you can start to share control you need to understand the nature of the dynamics you are up against. I refer to these dynamics as Job Search Forces. These forces include motivation, activity and being realistic. They are linked closely together and can easily be out of balance, if they are not monitored.

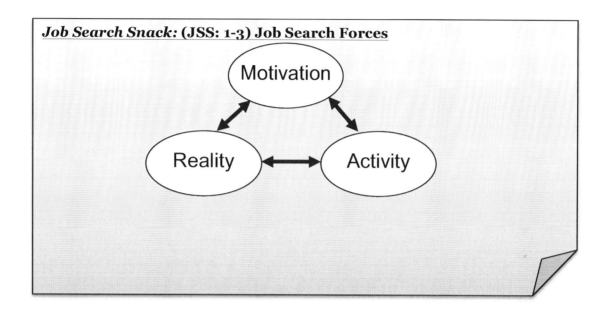

3. Understanding the Job Search Forces

In my office I have a sign posted that all my clients can easily see when they come in for a meeting.

The sign reads:

If your *motivation* is not high, you are less likely to have high job search *activity*.

If you have low job search *activity*, you cannot be *realistic* about your job chances.

If you're not *realistic* about your job chances, you're less likely to have high *motivation* to continue your job search.

Therefore...

By maintaining your motivation, you will increase your job search activity.

By maintaining your job search activity, you will have more realistic expectations.

By maintaining reasonable expectations, you will remain motivated.

Having worked with adults of all ages, at various times of their careers, I have faced the challenge of helping them to maintain their level of motivation. Motivation is a very subjective concept that varies from person to person. The need to identify what motivates you to find a job, however, is not really important to the Job Search Process. What is important to understand is that you can maintain a high level of motivation by concentrating on other aspects of your job search. For example, imagine you've just started your job search. Your resume is up-to-date and your interview skills are sharper than ever.

Job Search Snack: **(JSS: 1-4) Job Search Ingredients that help to manage Job Search Forces**

Job Search Ingredient	The Job Search Force Managed	Page of Job Search Ingredient
1. Job Search Numbers	Activity	Page 54
2. The who, what, when, where and why	Motivation	Page 66
3. The Hiring Cycle	Reality Motivation	Page 81
4. The Next Step	Reality Motivation	Page 92
5. The Job Search Process	Activity Motivation Reality	Page 100

Each morning you scour the daily newspaper for employment opportunities. You've identified a few job opportunities that match your skills and experience, and you apply for those jobs. At the end of the week you haven't received any calls for interviews, so you tell yourself that it is okay because you figure the employers probably require some time to go over all the resumes they have received. You decide to continue to do what you have been doing. As we said earlier, the more resumes you send out, the greater the likelihood of finding a job, right? After all, if you were to apply to every job you came across, you'd be bound to get an interview, even if merely by accident. (This is assuming that your resume is well written or your ability to complete an employment application form is acceptable, of course). However, if you were to continue at this pace of submitting resumes or filling out applications without receiving a phone call, then it would be understandable that your motivation to continue would gradually lessen. It's human nature to feel defeated if we continue to try something with little success. This is why it is important to understand the job search odds. If you aware and you are able to estimate the odds of a particular employment opportunity, your likelihood of maintaining your motivation will increase. For example, when we play the lotto our expectations are reasonably low with regards to winning the grand prize, because if they weren't we wouldn't be in the habit of purchasing tickets on a regular basis. We've basically programmed ourselves to accept the fact that buying lotto tickets is a chance to win a great amount of money, but we understand that the reality of taking the money home is highly unlikely; therefore, when we don't win, we are not that disappointed. We invariably continue to buy the tickets just in case our ticket numbers do come up, because if we don't play, we simply don't have a chance of winning. This is an important lesson when we job search: If we don't submit resumes or fill out applications, there is no chance of getting the job. As long as we know the odds, the way we deal with the rejection of not getting an interview will not be as severe. Of course, the good news is that the odds are better than playing the lotto! Take a look at the following chart and examine how the odds affect what we expect in certain situations.

The example of the lotto tickets will help you understand the dynamics of the job search and the importance, therefore, of playing the job search odds. As identified in the **Playing the Job Search Odds** chart above, applying to a posting whereby you have a limited number of skills required for the position gives you a slim chance of getting that job. While I would not discourage anyone from applying for a job even when they are not qualified, I would make the point that the odds of getting the job are very low, and that they most likely should simply submit a "generic resume" and to not waste too much time and energy. If you can understand the odds, the impact it will have on you when you don't receive a call for an interview will not be as great. Therefore, your motivation level will not be as badly affected and your approach to a realistic job search will be maintained. The Job Search Forces, once understood, will help you deal with the dynamics that affect your ability to secure employment.

Now let's look at each of the Job Search Forces a little more closely...

Reality: Maintaining a realistic outlook

Maintaining a realistic outlook during your job search is critical as you continue to look for work. If you are qualified to be a chemist, then any job posting involving a chemist position may be realistic. However, if you are not qualified to be a chemist, applying to this type of position may not be realistic. This is an over-simplification, but it serves our purposes well. The key here is to remember to maintain a realistic approach to looking for work. If you are not realistic, the chances of finding employment are drastically reduced. The reasons you want to find employment quickly are quite personal, but for the purpose of this book the goal of finding employment quickly can only be accomplished if you remain positive in your job search as long as possible. If you continue to apply to jobs for which you are neither qualified nor possess the required experience, you are taking an unrealistic approach in your job search. A result of being unrealistic is the negative impact upon your motivation and your drive to continue looking for work.

If you want to determine how realistic you are being, there are a number of things that you can do. First, you probably ought to speak with a job search coach. These individuals are trained to provide assistance and guidance, and can act as a sounding board. You probably also should speak to some employers prior to actually applying for the opportunity (we'll review this in greater detail later on in the book). The things you do to determine if you are being realistic are critical.

Taste Test: (TT: 1-1) The Realistic Job Search - Understanding the job search odds

Below is an example of a job seeker's profile and a number of job opportunities. Based on the profile and information in the job opportunity, try to determine which job opportunity is the most realistic for the job seeker.

Job Seeker Profile

Type of job seeking: -Looking for work as a salesperson.

Education: - College degree in Marketing

                        - Certificate in sales

Age: 22

Work History: He has had a number of full-time summer jobs working in construction and one summer working at a call centre. He is presently volunteering as a tutor, teaching residents how to read.

Skills and abilities: Computer literate, excellent interpersonal skills, strong team player

*Answers can be found on pages 201-203. *

Sample Job Opportunities

*Job Opportunity #1 – Newspaper Ad

Customer Service Representative

Working in our Commodities Trading department, with emphasis on excellent customer service, the responsibilities for this position require the processing of sales orders and customer inquiries in a timely, efficient, and proactive manner. The successful candidate will: enter sales contracts; schedule shipments; answer customer inquiries regarding invoice/contract details, load-order status, contract position, and unpriced product; generate invoices and prepare sales reports; and ensure credit and inventory issues are properly addressed.

Qualified candidates will possess a post-secondary business diploma and have two (2) years experience in a sales-related environment with a demonstrated aptitude for superior customer service. Proficiency with PC applications such as Word and Excel is required, and experience with SAP would be an asset.

Qualified candidates should forward a resume no later than September 17, 2006.

Beth Armstrong
XYZ Company
3456 Somewhere Street
beth.armstrong@xyzcompany.com

Job Opportunity #2 – Verbal Job Lead

> ### Job Opportunity for an Inside Sales Representative position from a friend of a friend
>
> A close friend of the individual advises them to call his friend to find out more about an opportunity for an Inside Sales Representative position. They give the friend a call and after introductions, the friend begins to talk about a position within her organization as an inside sales representative. She is the assistant to the sales manager that will do the interviewing. The position requires some experience in sales, computer skills and access to a vehicle. The assistant provides the individual with the manager's name and phone number, and suggests that they use her name as a reference when they submit their resume.

Job Opportunity #3 – Cold Call

> ### Cold call at a Telecommunications company – Human Resource Department
>
> The individual calls up a large telecommunications company and is directed to their human resource department. She asks if the company is hiring in any of their sales departments. The HR person provides them with an email where they can submit their resume for an opening. However, they are not sure about the specific positions they may have in the sales department.

***Job Search Snack:* (JSS: 1-5) Are you realistic?**

Here are some indicators that may help you to determine if you are being realistic:

- Type of jobs you are applying for

- Are you entering the Hiring Cycle at the right time (See Ingredient #3: The Hiring Cycle)

- The number of contacts in your network (See Stage One: Identifying Opportunities)

- Understanding the labor market

- Matching skills/experience to the job opportunity

- Knowing the next step

***Job Search Activity:* (JSA: 1-2) Past job opportunities**

Think of the last couple of jobs you have applied for and write down what the position required. Be as specific as possible and determine whether your skills, background and present situation matched what the employer was looking for. If you have not been actively looking for work, take an existing job posting that you would be interested in and determine if your skills and background match the requirements.

===

Motivation: Staying motivated throughout the Job Search Process

Motivation is an important factor in losing weight, quitting smoking or looking for a job. This is the most difficult of all the Job Search Forces. Your motivation to look for work will come in many different forms. The key here is to identify what makes you want to wake up in the morning and look for a job, while at the same time maintaining a realistic approach and level of activity that will lead to your success. There are many motivational programs on the market today that can help you during your job search. Ask a friend or speak to a job search

Manage your activity and a realistic outlook on your chances of getting a job .

coach for suggestions. However, if you choose not to follow a motivational program, keep in mind that the key to conducting a job search is to ensure that you are active and have a plan that will lead to success. The Job Search Management Recipe introduced in this book will provide you with a job search framework, so you can maintain a structured approach while you look for work.

The key to maintaining a level of motivation that will help you through the Job Search Process is to manage your activity and a realistic outlook on your chances of getting a job. If you are working with a job search professional, a friend or family member, they can help you to determine if you are doing the right things. Staying motivated can only be accomplished through doing the right things, because you will otherwise become dejected very quickly. Rejection is a major part of the job search, and in order to deal with it effectively, you must be realistic about every job opportunity.

Job Search Snack: (JSS: 1-6) How do you know if you're still motivated?

Here are some indicators of your motivational level:

- Intrinsic – you need a challenge

- Extrinsic – you need money

- The quality of your daily routine

- The strength of your positive versus your negative behaviors

- You possess a strong network

- Your understanding of the Hiring Cycle

- Your ability to gather information

- Your effective playing of the job search odds

Job Search Activity: (JSA: 1-3) What motivates you?

What motivates you? Do you need or want a job? When you are feeling down, what picks you up again? Answer these questions and write down everything that motivates you. Once you've identified the things that motivate you, indicate which ones are realistic with an asterisk (*).

_____

_____

_____

_____

_____

_____

_____

_____

_____

Activity: Maintaining an appropriate level of job search activity

I've worked with many job search clients who have found a job purely by accident. They just happened to be in the right place at the right time. I have always wondered why some of my clients have been able to find work this way. I kept coming back to the same reason: activity. Those clients who had a high level of activity would always secure a job regardless of their background. The more activity involving actually looking for employment the higher your chances of finding a job. This seems like common sense, but you would be surprised how few job seekers are able to maintain a level of activity that leads to a positive outcome. A realistic approach to their job search was missing, which in turn decreased their motivation, resulting in an even further reduction of activity.

Putting a plan together that ensures you have a sufficient level of activity is absolutely critical to your job search success. The level of your job search activity will determine whether or not you will be able to maintain the motivation required to conduct an effective job search. In addition, you need to be realistic about your chances of getting <u>each</u> job you apply for and not just your overall job search chances. This is an important distinction to make. If you look for work thinking that you have a realistic chance of getting a job because the industry requires new employees, you may overlook specific risks to the employer regarding hiring you. By assessing each job opportunity (see JSA: 2-5) you will be more likely to continue your activity.

Job Search Snack: (JSS: 1-7) When activity is low

Here are some indicators of job search inactivity:

- Low motivation

- Not knowing your job search numbers

- Poor time management

- Limited employer cold calls

- No structure to the job search

- Inability to gather job-related information

- Not increasing the number of contacts in your network

- Not realistic about job search chances

- Only applying to newspaper or online job ads

Job Search Activity: *(JSA: 1-4) What do I do during the day?*

Write down your daily activities. Start with when you wake up in the morning until the time you go to bed. When do you watch TV, conduct your job search, and how much time do you spend surfing the Internet? Be as specific as you can.

_____

_____

_____

_____

_____

_____

_____

_____

_____

_____

_____

_____

Dealing with the Job Search Forces and Control

The activities that you have completed regarding each of the Job Search Forces will allow you to identify some of the behavioural patterns that exist in your life. The key to looking for employment is your ability to modify the way that you approach life. We have all heard that looking for work is a fulltime job. Well, looking for a job is somewhat like being employed. Regardless, the key to a successful job search is that you are able to identify the things you are doing well versus those that are causing difficulty, so that you can find employment as quickly as possible. The Job Search Forces must be understood in order for you to deal with the challenges to be faced during the Job Search Process. If you can understand what impacts you, you are in a better position to work through the difficult stages of looking for work. I've found that if my clients can articulate what they experience, they are better at dealing with the trials and tribulations of their job search. If you are able to understand the Job Search Forces, you will be in a better position of control throughout the Job Search Process. The notion of control is central to an effective approach, when dealing with employers. It's not a simple concept, but the more you manage the Job Search Forces, the easier it will become to take control of your interactions with employers. At times, this might not be possible for you to do on your own. You may consider working with a job search coach or career counsellor who can help you along this path.

<u>***Taste Test:*** **(TT: 1-2) Job Search Forces and Control**</u>

1. What are the three forces that you need to manage during your job search?

    _____   _____   _____

2. What is the best way to maintain your motivation throughout the Job Search Process?

    _____

    _____

    _____

    _____

3. What is the best way to share control in the Job Search Process? (Circle all that are

    appropriate)

    a. Tell employers your conducting a job search

    b. Share control with employers

    c. Make sure to gather enough information

    d. Be prepared

4. Why are the odds of getting a job from a newspaper ad very low?

    _____

    _____

    _____

5. When putting together an Action Plan, it is important to have a Plan B in case there is

not an opportunity to achieve Plan A. Plan B should be linked to Plan A, and should focus

not necessarily on the job, but the type of organization.

    True   False

    *Answers can be found on pages 201-203. *

PART TWO: THE JOB SEARCH INGREDIENTS

What are the Job Search Ingredients?

Just like any good recipe, the quality of the ingredients helps determine the outcome of the dish. Your job search won't be any different. The quality of your approach to finding employment, within a reasonable amount of time, will depend on your ability to move through the Job Search Process efficiently. To be able to do this you will require an understanding of how the Job Search Process works and how you can manoeuvre through it as easily as possible. (In Part Two, we will review each of the Job Search Ingredients in detail.) The Job Search Ingredients include:

1. **Job Search Numbers**

2. **The What, Who, When, Where and Why**

3. **The Hiring Cycle**

4. **The Next Step**

5. **The Job Search Process**

INGREDIENT 1'

INGREDIENT #1: JOB SEARCH NUMBERS

*(Deals with Job Search Force **Activity**)*

Why we Collect Statistics

Statistics are a way of understanding a particular situation. They allow us to generate questions as to why certain things are the way they are. For example, a census provides

government with a portrait of the individuals who live in a certain area or region. From this census data, they are able to determine what the profile is and how they could better serve the people. Collecting job search statistics will allow you to identify things that you are doing well, and those things you are doing poorly. If we can isolate the behaviours that are negatively affecting our job search, we can then eliminate them in terms of the way we look for work in order to better increase our chances of finding a job. In addition to helping yourself identify specific issues, identifying these behaviours will also help your job search coach, employment counsellor or career practitioner to understand what you are doing during your job search, and how they can therefore help you to do it better.

Looking at your Job Search Numbers

What you're about to read may fly in the face of every other job search book or coach's opinion out there, but in my experience, looking at the job search numbers (or the amount of jobs applied to) is extremely important, especially when you start looking for a job. Targeting your search toward specific jobs that match your skills and abilities is said by some to be the most productive use of your job search time. Although I cannot disagree with this approach, I think it is important that you also submit as many resumes as you can. Let me clarify. When conducting your job search, you need to divide it into two separate approaches. One is the **targeted approach** and the other is the ***passive approach***. Each of these approaches has their own benefits and should be dealt with in entirely different ways. The targeted approach deals with linking job opportunities to your skills, abilities and experience. The

targeted approach also involves a lot of time and so the number of opportunities may not be as great as the passive approach. The passive approach involves randomly sending out resumes to as many job opportunities as possible as long as the job lead relates to your employment goal. I recommend this approach early on in your job search, because it is usually at this stage that you are just beginning to gather targeted job leads. The passive approach does not take much effort to conduct and expectations should not be that high. Maintaining a significant level of activity early on in the job search is critical to your success. Although the passive approach is by no means the most effective, it will provide you with a psychological edge in that you are able to witness yourself engaged in some real job search activity. The targeted approach, although more effective, takes longer to conduct and can be sometimes disenchanting to seekers who do not see any immediate return on their effort.

As you read through the following pages, keep both the targeted and passive approach in the back of your mind. Otherwise, if you remain simply focused on targeted resumes only, your job search numbers will not look the same as someone who is applying to as many job leads as possible. What's important here is that you find a balance between the two approaches. You need to become knowledgeable of your chances for each job opportunity, which in turn, will ultimately determine the most effective job search numbers for you.

Let's say you have applied for 50 jobs, over the last two (2) months. On average, there are 30 days in a month and let's say 20 business days. That means in the last two months you have had 40 business days to identify job opportunities and submit resumes. If you have submitted 50 resumes over that time period that gives you roughly 1.25 submissions per day. Is this

enough? As noted earlier, I know you've probably heard from many people that looking for employment is a full time job! If it is a full time job and you have only submitted 1.25 resumes per day, and each resume takes about ten (10) minutes, then you're only working 60 minutes a week. That doesn't seem full-time, does it? Multiply the number of jobs you have applied for in the last little while by 10. If the original number of submissions was 50, you now have submitted 500. This works out to six (6) submissions a day. Just by doing the math we can see that by increasing your activity, you increase the number of job opportunities that may become available to you. Of course, in some areas of the country it may not be possible to increase the number of resumes you submit (for example, if you're living in a small rural area the approach may be a little different). Geography aside, the benefit of increasing the number of resumes you submit is hard to ignore. Regardless, managing your job search uses the exact same principles that will be discussed in forthcoming sections where we will discuss different approaches to increasing the chances of getting you that perfect job.

The point I want to make here is that ***activity*** is the key to looking for and securing employment. If your job search activity is low, then your likelihood of finding employment is also low. When people say that looking for employment is a full-time job, they usually don't know how to tell you what they actually mean by "full-time". In my opinion, job searching as a full-time job is a universal concept; the number of hours an individual works is just different.

This book will attempt to address the notion of job searching being full-time, by presenting a job search management approach that will allow you to both manage and organize your job search, by providing a framework that will guide you through the process on a daily basis.

Job Search Snack: **(JSS: 2-1) The Targeted Approach vs. the Passive Approach to the Job Search Process**

Positives	Positives
• Greater odds of getting the job	• Increased odds of getting job using a "blanket" approach to applying
• Typically tied to a referral, which increases the chances of getting an interview	• Less time invested per job opportunity
• Directed to a specific individual	• Limited effort required (using passive resume form)
• Sourcing job opportunities requires research	• Limited energy spent per application (otherwise sounds like a repeat of 2nd one)
• Following-up is possible	
• Can contact employer prior to resume submission	
• Higher quality job potential	

Challenges	Challenges
• Substantial time investment	• Lower odds of getting a job
• Longer Hiring Cycle	• Can hurt motivation if realistic expectations are not set at the beginning
• A lot of energy invested per job opportunity	• Little information about opportunities are available
	• Not necessarily the perfect job match

What are my Job Search Numbers?

How many job opportunities have you identified in the last week? How many jobs have you applied for in the last week? How many interviews have you been called for during the last week? These are questions that are critical to your job search success. Knowing these numbers allows you to monitor your progress and daily activity. Suppose that you have identified 30 job opportunities, have applied to 18, and are scheduled for one interview. It would look something like this:

Job Opportunities	Applications	Set Interviews
30	18	1

Looking at the numbers allows us to do a couple of things and forces us to ask a couple of questions. The first question would be: *"Why have you only identified 30 job opportunities?"* Not that this is necessarily a poor or low number; I just should know why the number is 30. In some rural areas this number may be appropriate because of the fewer opportunities available. Due to the limited number of job opportunities in specific industries this number may also be an acceptable amount. However, the same number in a large urban centre or within some industries may be too low. An individual may also be targeting specific companies, which reduces the numbers substantially. Whatever the number, we should always question ourselves as to why the number is what it is. The number of opportunities we identify is directly related to our Job Search Process. In Section 2 we will look more closely at various ways to identify job opportunities. If you are working with a counsellor or job search facilitator, then this number will provide them with valuable insight into your ability or **inability** to generate job leads. If the number is too low, focus may be put on how you are identifying employment opportunities.

The next question you would have to ask yourself is why you have only applied to 18 of the 30 opportunities. What happened to the other 12 opportunities? I've heard a number of different answers to this question. It always depended on the individual with whom I was working. Even when they gave me an answer, it didn't really matter; it was the individual's job search number, not mine. However, it should matter to the individual why there is a discrepancy between the identified opportunities and the number of resumes or applications submitted. Let's consider some possible answers. The most obvious answer could be that the deadline for applications had expired for some of the job leads identified. Another obvious answer is that the job opportunity turned out to be the wrong position they were looking for. Perhaps the individual simply forgot to submit an application. Whatever the question and whatever the answer, the point of the exercise is to identify the activity or the lack of activity and to start to develop a job search profile.

Say that you identified 30 opportunities and applied to 18. You received a call for one (1) interview. What does this mean? If you looked at the numbers you would probably say that this was not good at all. However, we need to consider a few factors before making this judgement. First of all, when were the 18 applications or resumes submitted? If they were submitted within the last couple of days, the number 18 is not a bad number at all. In most cases, employers wait until they have collected a number of resumes before they start to contact people for interviews. Also, if there were application deadlines (which means the employer waits for a certain date before conducting interviews), this may also explain the reason for the low number. On the other hand, if the 18 applications had been submitted two weeks prior, this is a different story. There still may be an application deadline for some of the opportunities, which is OK. Those that were without application deadlines require a next step (we'll get into more detail regarding generating the next step in Section 2). The question therefore becomes, what can you do to find out if any of the 17 remaining opportunities are going to move forward in the Job Search Process.

Using our Job Search Numbers to move us through the Job Search Process

Observing these numbers allows us to proactively monitor our Job Search Process and identify weaknesses in our approach. What is the reason for collecting statistics? Simply put, statistics allow us to see the whole picture of a given situation. By collecting job search numbers, we obtain the ability to reflect on what we have been doing. We noted earlier the expression: "Looking for work is a full-time job". In some cases your numbers will not look the way you thought they should, and you may require professional assistance. If you do seek assistance, you will be able to share your numbers with your counsellor who may, in turn, see something differently than you do. A plan of action could then be created to determine the best way of moving you through the Job Search Process. Also, by collecting job search

> *The number of opportunities we identify is directly related to our Job Search Process.*

statistics you will be able to ascertain the amount of effort you are putting into looking for work. If you decide to set targets for the number of job opportunities you are going to identify on a weekly basis, this then structures the time you spend looking for work. Just like how you would work from 9 to 5 at a regular job, you now know that, at the very minimum, you will be working towards your targets. Whether it takes 12 or 20 hours to meet your targets doesn't really matter. The point is that you now have a reason to 'punch in', and then to 'punch out' when you have met your job search targets.

An exercise that I commonly do with individual clients or groups is to have everyone give me their three job search numbers at the beginning of a job search session. If I were working with a group of job seekers, I would get everyone to put their three numbers on a flipchart at the beginning of each workshop. There are no names beside the numbers so no one can be singled out. Once all the numbers are written down, I ask the class to analyze them. Individuals are often amazed at some of the suggestions they receive when other individuals analyze their numbers. This could work for you, as well. Collect your numbers and share them with your spouse, partner, friend or a family member. Get them to ask you questions regarding your activity, even if they don't know anything about what the numbers represent. A useful dialogue will then emerge, and through this dialogue you start to get different opinions about your job search approach. Avoid being defensive, but view this as an opportunity to gather information.

How do I start to collect my numbers and how often?

Every time you identify a job opportunity, record it on a piece of paper, in a journal, on a spreadsheet, or wherever you know your number will be safely recorded (**note**: *if you have an account at* www.snagpad.com, *these numbers will automatically be recorded for you as you add job opportunities*). Make sure to put a date beside the opportunity. The layout could look something like this:

Date	Job Opportunity	Approach	Applied	Set Interviews

It is important that you write down the date on which the opportunity was identified. Understanding the Hiring Cycle (Ingredient #2) is an important aspect of gathering your numbers and knowing what to with them. Each opportunity is date driven and there are expiration dates to each job lead. What you should do is monitor your activity, so that you can make any corrective actions down the road. The numbers will allow you to determine what you are doing well in your job search and what needs improvement. As you continue through the sections of this book, you will discover that there are stages to the Job Search Process. Each of these stages has different, yet required techniques that are designed to increase your chances of being successful in your job search. By breaking each of these stages down, you will not feel overwhelmed, which one can feel at times when looking for work.

Sharing your Job Search Numbers

Sharing your job search numbers with others will provide you with additional insight into what you are doing during your job search. Through the use of a job search management network, I have been able to work with a number of clients who have supported each other. In a typical group, whenever we would meet, I would have each of the participants write their three job search numbers on a flipchart prior to entering the classroom. Once all of the participants had written down their numbers, we would take turns assessing each of them. The beauty of this feedback process was that when they wrote their numbers on the flipchart, no one would know whose numbers they were, because there would be no name beside them. The following is a sample list of job search numbers for a group of ten job seekers.

O (Job Opportunities)	A (Applied)	I (Interviews)
22	20	2
15	14	1
5	2	0
8	5	0
2	1	1
40	35	3
19	10	3
24	21	0
50	40	0
12	8	1

If we examine these numbers without knowing anything about the individual, and where the only information that we have is that these numbers represent activity over the last seven days, what could we say about them? Let's look at the Job Opportunity column. Who would have the best numbers in this column? One might think that the larger the number of job opportunities the better the chances for employment. This may not necessarily be true in all cases. Just because an individual has identified 50 job opportunities does not mean that they are good quality. You should know what the 50 job opportunities represent and find out where they came from. An opportunity from a newspaper ad may not have the same value as an opportunity from a referral. It all depends on the source and how the individual's qualifications match up against the requirements of the opportunity. Looking at the Job Opportunities column alone may not give us that much information, but it does at least allow us to ask questions about them.

If we turn our attention to the Application column, we can now start to look at the relationship between this column and Job Opportunity column in order to help us determine the effectiveness of these numbers. Let's look again at the row with 50 job opportunities in it. You can see that a large number of opportunities have been identified and, of those, the individual has applied to 40. The first obvious question would be: *What happened to the other ten (10) job opportunities? Why hadn't the individual applied to those?* A possibility could be that the deadline for submitting the application had not yet arrived, and that the individual was in the process of gathering more information, so they could customize their resume. It is also possible that the job opportunities did not work out, as the job seeker may not have had the appropriate qualifications. These are just a few possible reasons. You can start to see that by just looking at the numbers we can start to analyze them, and this could provide information that can help the job seeker through the Job Search Process.

Finally, let's look at the last column. The number of Set Interviews may reflect a number of factors. First of all, it is possible that the deadline for applications has not arrived and there is a time delay. If this were the case, I would want to make sure that the individual was aware of the deadline, and could comment if they had not received a call for an interview. The job seeker's response could either be: that she originally determined her chances for getting the interview were low to begin with; or that she, indeed, thought she had a good chance of getting the interview and, accordingly, now needs to contact the employer to find out why she hasn't been contacted. It is also possible that the reason the individual is not getting calls for interviews is because of his resume. I would want to have another look at the person's resume to determine if the resume matches the type of jobs the individual is applying to. Another possibility is that the opportunities the person is identifying do not fall in line with his skills or qualifications. I would then want to revisit their Action Plan to see whether it has changed. Whatever the reason, the point here is to raise these questions so that you can start to determine possible reasons for you are not moving through the Job Search Process.

Now that we have gone through each of the columns, we can see that looking at numbers in isolation does not provide the total picture we need. By looking at the relationship between the columns, we can start to determine where changes are needed in order to move us along in the Job Search Process. If our numbers are 50-40-0 they may appear to be inadequate.

However, if we've ruled out that there is not a time element, we can start to analyze them to determine ways of increasing the number of opportunities in the Set Interview column.

If you are looking for work on your own, it is a good idea to collect job search numbers so that you can assess where you have been, and where you still need to go. By reviewing your numbers on a regular basis, you will ensure that you are not repeating the same mistakes with each job opportunity.

Taste Test: (TT: 2-1) Job Search Numbers

1. What are the three numbers that are important to track during your job search?

    _____   _____   _____

2. Why is it important to collect job search numbers?

    _____

    _____

    _____

3. What are the benefits of taking a "targeted approach" to your job search?

    _____

    _____

    _____

    _____

4. What are the benefits of taking a "passive approach" to your job search? What are the challenges?

    _____

    _____

    _____

5. What would you say about these particular job search numbers: *15, 7, 1*

    _____

    _____

    Answers can be found on pages 201-203. *

INGREDIENT #2: THE WHAT, WHO, WHERE, WHEN AND WHY

*(Examines Job Search Force: **Motivation**)*

Focusing on what you're doing during the job search

As an employment counsellor, one of my main responsibilities was to identify the needs of the client with whom I was working. You can imagine how difficult it was to determine what my clients needed when they themselves had a hard time explaining it. However, we both knew that the ultimate need was: a job. I realized that it wasn't necessary to dwell on what my client needed, but to focus more specifically on what the individual was doing with regards to their job search. Remember, when a person is looking for a job, it is assumed that they have an Action Plan in place, including: knowing what type of field they want to work in; they have a cover letter and resume; they've practiced their interview skills, and are mentally prepared to begin their job search. By taking this approach, I was able to develop a conversation between my client and myself with regard to any issues that could adversely affect their ability to secure employment. During your job search you'll be confronted with many different challenges affecting your ability to find employment. In order to propel yourself forward through these challenging times, it is important that you understand what you are doing with regard to your job search activity and determine what is working and what is not.

By focusing on what you do rather than what you need, you'll start to gain the skills necessary to identify specific issues affecting your movement through the Job Search Process. Even if you identify something that you are doing that you know is not productive, you could either try to deal with it yourself, seek a family member or friend's advice, or go and see an employment or career counsellor. This approach allows you to work on specific issues affecting your ability to move forward in the Job Search Process. Don't dwell on what you need, because it is already obvious. Instead, *focus on what you are doing.* It's more efficient and will provide you with the insight necessary to understand how you are doing in your job search.

Determining what you do

One question you should ask yourself is: What do I do on any given day in terms of my job search activity? Let's take Monday as an example. When you wake up in the morning, what is the first thing that you do? For example, you wake up, go and take a shower, brush your teeth, comb your hair and get dressed. You then eat breakfast while reading the morning newspaper. After you finish reading the paper, you go to your computer to retrieve emails and look at the different job-related websites for any new opportunities. This may seem like a mundane task, but the importance lies in the ability for you to examine what you do with your time. If looking for a job is full-time, what specifically do you do with your time? In the following Job Search Activity form, write down exactly what you do from the moment you wake-up to the time you go to bed in the evening.

Job Search Activity: (JSA: 2-1) Daily Activities Form

1._____ 11._____

2._____ 12._____

3._____ 13._____

4._____ 14._____

5._____ 15._____

6._____ 16._____

7._____ 17._____

8._____ 18._____

9._____ 19._____

10._____ 20._____

Once you have created a list of activities you perform on a daily basis, go back to the list and write down beside each activity whether it is job search related (JS) or non job search related (NJS). You then should look at the distribution of activities associated with JS and NJS. Do NJS activities account for more than JS activities? If so, why? You probably should ask yourself if this is the best way to conduct a productive job search.

After you have completed the daily activity list you should be able to see a pattern in your routine. Most of my clients would quickly see that the number of job search activities they were conducting was inadequate for a typical day. It is important that you find a balance in the activities you conduct during your job search. Let's consider, as an example, the situation where the majority of your activities were non-job search related. The question then becomes: How do we know that we have a proportionate balance among our activities?

What does your job search activity presently consist of?

Determine what is working and what is not.

We've already discussed that the amount of job search activity you conduct increases your likelihood of finding a job. The key to increasing your activity is determining whether the activity you are doing is productive. In order to determine the level of your productivity, you must understand what it means to be productive during a job search. First of all, you must ask yourself: How many people know that you are looking for a job? Sharing your Job Search Process with family, friends and acquaintances will help you on many levels. Human beings are generally understanding and compassionate toward others. You may know of an individual who is not, but in my experience if we give people a chance, their willingness to help usually shines through. Emotional support and possibly financial support are the two main issues at stake when you don't share your job search with others. A job search can be a long and frustrating experience, and if you're not willing to seek support then it will become even more difficult. You're probably asking what this has to do with your activities. The key to any job search is building a support system around you. The question then becomes: How are you presently doing this? Over the years I have encouraged my clients to look closely at their interactions with people in their lives at the time of their job search.

Each individual in our lives can help in some way or another and we need to identify, among the people we know, what they can do. This may sound like taking advantage of an individual, but look at it more as an opportunity to get to know the individual. Moreover, if the person is ever in the same situation, you can be there for them. If you make this promise to yourself and intend on following through with it, you'll feel better about yourself and strive to make more connections.

As was mentioned earlier, the more contacts you make the greater the likelihood that you will come across some job-related information. The activities that you perform on a regular basis determine the number and type of contacts you will make. What I would like you to do now is take the activities that you identified from the **_Job Search Activity:_** (JSA: 2-1) Daily Activities Form and indicate the number of people you know who could become involved in that activity. If the activity is something that you can do alone, write "o" beside it.

Job Search Activity: (JSA: 2-2) Daily Activities with Others Form

1._____ _____   11._____ _____

2._____ _____   12._____ _____

3._____ _____   13._____ _____

4._____ _____   14._____ _____

5._____ _____   15._____ _____

6._____ _____   16._____ _____

7._____ _____   17._____ _____

8._____   _____   18._____   _____

9._____   _____   19._____   _____

10._____   _____   20._____   _____

===

Who's involved in your Job Search?

Now that you've identified the number of people who could be involved in your activities, you ought to look at all the activities that have "0" beside them. Some of these activities will have to continue as they are, such as brushing your teeth or eating breakfast. However, if you have indicated that you are creating resumes or practicing your interview skills on your own, you may wish to consider looking for help. A job coach, employment counsellor, family member or friend could all be good sources of assistance regarding this activity. Yes, you could easily do this on your own. However, the practice of doing it with someone else will provide the potential support you require to develop your skills. More importantly, it will help you to maintain your motivation throughout the Job Search Process. Also, if you are able to get others to see what you are doing, they may see some things that you do not and could potentially help you to improve your approach.

The simple exercise of identifying the activities you perform on a regular basis is important to moving you through the Job Search process. The activities you perform are directly correlated to your motivation, and if you are not doing things that are productive to your job search, your willingness to continue will dramatically decrease. Identifying what you're "doing" during your job search is the most effective way to determine that which you are doing well and what you need to improve upon. We all know what you need, but how you get there is the key to success.

I want to give you an example of a client I worked with that continually focused on what she needed – a job. By doing this she actually hurt herself because she was so intently focused on getting a job that she lost focus on how she was going to obtain one. In working with clients, the measurement of my success was based on whether or not they found employment. If you want to talk about pressure, an employment counsellor is right up there with the toughest of professions. I realized early on in my career that if I simply focused on the end result and threw in some resume writing and interview skills, everything would not work out as I planned. Let me illustrate what I mean with an example.

The activities you perform are directly correlated to your motivation.

One of my clients (I will call her Jane) with whom I had been working for a couple of weeks was seeking work as a secretary. Jane was a single mother with two small children. Both children were still at home and, because of Jane's employment status, she was able to care for them herself. Jane had been collecting employment insurance benefits for the preceding four (4) months. She required a job as her benefits were soon to run out. Her mother was able to care for the children a couple hours each day, while Jane was looking for a job. My usual practice, once I take on a client, is to let them continue to look for work on their own for a week or so. My goal is to see what kind of job search activity they are doing and to determine their motivational level. Of course,

I would initially spend some time determining their career goals, the type of job they are looking for and whether their resume and cover letter was in good shape or not. Jane appeared to have everything in order. Her resume was well done, and she had even had a professional resume writing service review it. We discussed the labor market conditions for secretaries, which at the time was moderate. At the end of the week, Jane came in to her scheduled appointment and sat down with me to discuss what had occurred throughout the week. During that time period, Jane had identified 20 job opportunities and applied to all of them either by faxing in a resume or filling out an application on-site. She had not received any calls at that point for interviews. This was understandable after only a week. We discussed her plans for the following week and she stressed to me again the importance to her finding a job as quickly as possible.

The following week, Jane brought in the same numbers. She had identified 20 job opportunities, applied to all of them and still had not received any calls from the previous week. In that two week period, Jane had identified a total of 40 job opportunities, applied to all of them, but did not receive one phone call. Jane and I discussed the possible reasons for why she had not received a call. We reviewed her resume again, which was strong, and decided that she would come back in a couple of days rather than a week to review her status. When Jane came in, she told me that she had identified 12 job opportunities and had applied to all of them. Better still, she had received one phone call from an employer. Unfortunately, Jane had to decline the interview because the job was at a place that manufactured plastic parts and Jane was allergic. So, after two and half weeks of conducting her job search, Jane had identified 45 job opportunities, applied to all 45 and received one call for an interview, which she could not attend. Given the number of job opportunities that Jane had identified, I felt she was on the right track. However, what worried me was that if Jane continued at this pace without any success, her motivational level would definitely drop, which then would affect her activity, and prevent her from being realistic about finding a job.

Making contacts to source employment is very important. Jane and I spent some time going over the type of job opportunities she was identifying, where she found the job leads, who she spoke to, and so on. As we started to talk about the job opportunities Jane identified, a pattern started to quickly emerge. The majority of the job leads were generated either through the newspaper or the Internet. There were a couple of opportunities identified through her local employment resource centre, and no leads were referred by anyone Jane knew. I have worked with clients who found employment through the newspaper or the Internet, but those opportunities were far and few between. It was interesting to see that Jane was generating her leads through these vehicles, which is not that unusual for job seekers to do. It became clear to me that if Jane continued to generate her leads through the newspaper and Internet, then it would continue to be difficult to get interviews. Why? The reason is that many people apply through these vehicles, yet the majority of job openings are not even advertised. What Jane needed to do was look for other sources of referrals. We began with Jane filling out the "Daily Activities Form". Once she had completed the form, an additional pattern emerged. The reason Jane was identifying job leads through the newspaper and on the Internet was that her mother had become ill and was no longer able to care for Jane's children. Jane had to stay home. Consequently, this was the easiest way to look for job leads.

After we discussed the limitations to this job search approach, Jane took her completed "Daily Activities Form" and looked for individuals she knew to help her with specific tasks. She identified a friend who was willing to come by her own house and look after the children for two hours a day. More important than that was Jane's discovery that the contacts she had who were already employed could provide potential job leads. The discovery of potential job leads through her family, friends and contacts, motivated her to tell as many people as she could that she was looking for work. Jane's job search took on a whole new approach, which included the addition of getting other individuals involved. For the first time, Jane realized that she was in a position to solicit the help of a number of different individuals, and not just myself, in her job search. By networking, Jane gained valuable job-related information that would assist her in the transition towards re-employment.

A few weeks later, Jane's job search numbers looked much different than they originally had. She continued to search the newspaper and Internet, but now, in addition to those two sources, she was utilizing the contacts she already possessed. Instead of identifying 20 job opportunities per week, Jane was identifying between 25-30 new job leads, with the majority coming through her contacts. The number of calls for interviews started to increase as well, due to the fact that the job referrals had more impact, because they were coming from someone the employer knew. This factor separated Jane from other candidates and provided her with an advantage. By the eighth week of our meetings, Jane was able to secure a job as a secretary with a company that she felt extremely excited about. Jane continues to grow her network, because she realizes that she may go through potential job changes, and now she understands the importance of making contacts to source employment.

Jane's story is not unique. Those job seekers who utilize or grow their networks typically find work much quicker and are extremely satisfied with the quality of the job that they find. The example of Jane's job search is an excellent illustration of why we must identify what activities in which you are involved during your job search. Before I could really help Jane, I needed to determine why she was not getting any interviews. The fact that she was only applying for jobs through the newspaper or on the Internet was the key to this. This put her at a significant disadvantage, because most job seekers use these means, causing greater competition. As well, Jane was missing out on opportunities unavailable through those two sources. Utilizing her network allowed Jane to expand her reach into the job market. Jane had finally entered the flow of job-related information.

Where are you Looking for Work?

If you're looking in the right place, your chances of finding work dramatically increase.

You also need to ask yourself where you are specifically looking for work. Where do most of your job leads come from? When I first meet clients and ask them this question, the typical response is "the newspaper or the Internet". I'm not surprised by this response. After all, it is the safest way to look for job leads. You do not have to leave the comfort of your home and you are looking at job opportunities that are real-time; you apply to a position that you know the employer is intending to fill immediately, unlike through a referral that may potentially take more time, because a position has to be created or one has to become available. It makes sense to look at these sources. However, only 15% of available job opportunities are identified this way. The majority of job opportunities are acquired through the "hidden" job market. What is the "hidden" job market? Basically, it is all available job opportunities that are not advertised in a paper or on the Internet. A lot of companies like to hire people that are referred by their existing employees. The simple reason for doing this is that if the employee who is referring the candidate is a good worker, it is likely that the individual they are referring is also a good worker. The goal of the employer is to eliminate the risk (see Section 2), and through referrals this can be accomplished.

Another reason why employers may not advertise through traditional sources could be because of their reputation. Often, large organizations have such good reputations for treating employees well that many people submit resumes to these companies. As a result, a large pool of potential workers already exists and if the right candidate can be found through the database, then there is no need to look elsewhere.

Also, the cost of placing an ad in the newspaper or on the Internet continues to rise and may not be cost effective for many companies. As a result of these growing costs, many employers are looking to their employees to provide referrals. In some larger companies, employees are compensated for referring an individual who is hired and remains employed for a period of time. The employee who is doing the referring is encouraged to refer someone who is able to perform; otherwise, they would not be rewarded. The company places value in these referrals and is more likely to hire someone who is referred from an existing employee. As a result of these practices, it has become more important for job seekers to build their networks in order to receive this type of job-related information. The longer you are out of work, the more likely you are not in the flow of this important information. The importance of building your network through volunteering, associations, and cold calling has never been more important.

Where you look for work is an important factor in determining not only if you find a job, but also how long it will take you to go through the Job Search Process. If you're looking in the right place, your chances of finding work dramatically increase. I'm not suggesting that you do not continue to look in the newspaper or on the Internet. However, by first evaluating where you are looking, you determine whether you are increasing your odds for getting an interview. Contacting an employer directly and utilizing contacts within your network will prove to be much more advantageous in terms of looking for work.

When are you Looking for Work?

Did you know that some industries, if you approached them during certain times of the day, would usher you out the door as quickly as you had walked in? A good example is the hospitality industry, which has peak busy periods throughout the day. Breakfast, lunch and dinner are considered the key time periods within this industry for generating profits. So, if a potential candidate were to just walk in during these periods, it would represent an obvious lack of knowledge about and consideration for the industry. This would shed a negative light on the individual. Obviously, this is a good example of why you must make sure that you approach opportunities at the right time, and that you should determine any time periods to avoid.

Let's look at a couple more examples of industries that are time-sensitive. If you were an accountant by profession and were looking for a new job, you should be careful how you go about applying during tax season. Most tax return companies are not terribly busy prior to the time individuals start to file their taxes. So if tax return deadlines typically begin in January and run through to the end of March, your job search timing must reflect this understanding. You should be looking for opportunities in October or November of the preceding year. However, you probably should also apply during the busy time as well, just in case the organization is still short-staffed. Therefore, you should listen to the news and get a sense of the labour market in order to make this judgement call regarding the timing. As well, the contacts within your network may provide you with some information on whether a company is hiring during a busy period.

Another example would be seasonal or project-based industries, such as retail, children's camps, educational institutions, IT, telecommunications and training. When applying to these industries, you need to consider the timeframe you have chosen when submitting your application, and what business cycle they may be in. This is critical to ensuring that your opportunity for success is increased. If you know people in these industries, they represent your link to information that may help you. If you don't know anyone, now is the time to start developing contacts. You should look to your network to find out if anyone knows of a contact that could help you.

The need to determine when you should be applying to specific job opportunities will encourage you to consider all of the possible factors that may be preventing you from getting an interview. The more aware you become of how the Job Search Process affects your chances for success, the more it will allow you to better manage the Job Search Forces. I've worked with many clients who felt that they had a great opportunity in terms of a job lead, and then proceeded to find out they did not even get the interview! In some instances, it was simply a case of the client not having the right skills or qualifications. In other situations, it was just the wrong time for the individual to enter the Job Search Process. Whatever the reason, the more you recognize what you are doing during the Job Search Process, the more likely you are to effectively deal with issues along the way.

Job Search Activity: (JSA: 2-3) Defining your Job Search Schedule

The first thing you need to do is identify the type of activities that make up your day. You've already done this on previous pages. For the purpose of this activity, let's break them up into two categories: one, personal activities (i.e., house cleaning, picking up the children, exercise);

and two, job search activities (i.e. research, resume updates, cold calls). In the table below, indicate all the activities with which you are presently involved during your week and list them on the lines provided.

Personal Activities	Job Search Activities

Now take each of your activities and put them in the appropriate time slot* in the schedule below.

Time*	Monday	Tuesday	Wednesday	Thursday	Friday
8:00 – 9:00					
9:00 – 10:00					
10:00 – 11:00					
11:00-12:00					
12:00 – 1:00					
1:00 – 2:00					
2:00 – 3:00					
3:00 – 4:00					
4:00 – 5:00					

Note: Time slots listed here are examples.

Now that you've identified the various activities that occupy your day, make an effort to follow the time lines. Initially there will be some tweaking and adjusting, but the key here is to provide the structure that will help motivate you in continuing your job search. The most important aspect in terms of scheduling your time is to ensure that you have tasks to perform on a regular basis. You may find that your job search activities only take up a small percentage of your overall activity. This is OK as long as you devote the designated time to your job search. Once you've completed your job search schedule you'll know when to punch in and punch out. The next time someone says, "Looking for work is a full-time job" you'll be able to tell him or her that you know exactly what they mean.

Why are you conducting your Job Search that way?

Now that you have identified what you are doing during your job search, you need to determine why you are doing it that way. Clients I have worked with over the years have conducted job searches for many years, but never really understood why they were doing it the way they were. If you tell a child to do something and they ask you why, they are more likely to finish the task if you are able to explain to them why you want the task completed. If they understand the "why" they are more apt to feel comfortable completing the task, because they are working with some purpose. The same goes for conducting a job search. If you know why you are doing something you are most likely in a better position to determine whether or not it is effective. If you are conducting your job search on your own, then be sure to have a discussion with a spouse, friend or family member and tell them what you are doing. The question you will find they naturally ask is: Why you are doing it that way? If you're working with a job search practitioner, be prepared to answer this question. Your answer will help shed light on your perceptions and ability to perform a successful job search.

Taste Test: (TT: 2-2) The What, Who, Where, When and Why

1. Why is it important to focus on what you're _doing_ during your job search, versus focusing on what you need?

_____

_____

_____

2. Describe what you are doing or plan to do for your own job search? (I.e., working with a job coach)

_____

_____

_____

_____

_____

3. Why have you chosen to conduct your job search in this way?

_____

_____

_____

_____

*Answers can be found on pages 201-203. *

INGREDIENT #3: THE HIRING CYCLE

*(Deals with the Job Search Forces: **Reality and Motivation**)*

What is the Hiring Cycle?

The most important yet least understood aspect of the job search is the Hiring Cycle. Most people forget when looking for a job that there are two parties involved: **the job searcher (i.e. you), and the employer**. If the employer is a part of the Job Search Process, then logically there has to be a timeframe associated with looking for a job. When I mention this to most people, they give me a funny look and say that this is pretty obvious. The fact of the matter is, it goes well beyond application deadlines and interview dates. Simply put, there are Hiring Cycles starting and ending everyday. Some companies have longer Hiring Cycles than others and its length usually depends on the type of job they are looking to fill. On average, the Hiring Cycle for an entry-level position is typically six to eight weeks. Does this surprise you? A survey conducted recently, of all types of companies, revealed that from the moment an organization posts an external opening, until an individual begins in that same position, the total timeframe is typically six to eight weeks. Of course there are exceptions, and positions can be filled the day they are posted or take three months.

My research has indicated, however, that the length of time to fill an entry-level position is, in fact, six to eight weeks. More specialized positions may take longer. I have spoken to individuals who have waited up to a year to go through the process of applying for a particular position. It really depends on the position and the company's hiring practice. The point is, as

job searchers, we have to be aware that time is always an issue. If we enter the position's Hiring Cycle towards the end, the likelihood of getting the position dramatically decreases. Given this knowledge, we need to manage the way we conduct our job search.

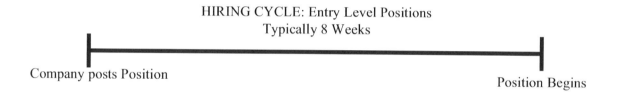

HIRING CYCLE: Entry Level Positions
Typically 8 Weeks

Company posts Position   Position Begins

For example, suppose you are applying for an entry-level position as a bank teller. You find out through a friend that the position is available and you are interested in getting the job. You prepare your resume, go down to the bank and drop it off. You are excited about this newfound opportunity and you eagerly await the call for the interview. After all, you're qualified, you have the right education for the position and you are a hard worker. Time passes and you still don't receive a call for an interview. You give the bank a call two weeks after submitting your resume, but the person on the other end of the line tells you that if you haven't received a call by now you will not be granted an interview. You are devastated. You have the right qualifications and education, and most of all you are willing to do anything to get this job. Your resume was perfect and the cover letter was customized for this position. What reasons could there be for not getting an interview?

There are a number of possible answers to this question. The most obvious one could be that there were many more qualified candidates, other than you. Unless you were the individual at the bank doing the screening process, you could never know whether or not this was the case. I like to refer to this possibility as the **unknowns**. Unless you know somebody within the bank, you are never going to find the answer. This is out of our control. Another possibility is that the bank was looking for specific qualifications that you did not possess, or that they were perhaps looking to hire women because they needed to meet gender equity quotas. Again, these are all **unknowns.** In my experience, you can drive yourself crazy trying to answer a question that really cannot be answered.

I like to offer a different possibility to my clients -- something that is more concrete. I refer to this as the **known**. Let's suppose that the bank decided that they required new tellers in January. By the time they got the approval to hire from upper management, they did not post the openings until the end of February. They wanted the new hires in training by the beginning of May, because a new branch was due to be opened at the end of May and they required all new staff members to be fully trained by that time. Since the training takes three weeks, it was important that all hiring decisions be made two to three weeks before May, in order to provide those individuals who were already working enough time to give notice to their existing employers. For that reason, they set the application deadline for April 10th. The bank would accept resumes after the 10th, but would grant them consideration only for a second round, and only if they did not find what they were looking for in the first round. Let's

say that you submitted your resume in the middle of April, making you part of the second round of resumes received. This puts you at a clear disadvantage for getting the job and decreases your chances.

Job Search Snack: **(JSS: 2-2) The known and unknown of the job search**

The nature of the job search is not knowing why your resume was not chosen for an interview. This is what we refer to as the unknown of the Job Search Process. In some cases you can find out information as to why you were not granted an interview, based on when you entered the Hiring Cycle. This is information that can be collected. The purpose of gathering this information is twofold. One, it will allow you to submit your resume prior to the deadline, and two, it can provide you with a possible reason as to why you were not selected for an interview, should it be the case that you entered the Hiring Cycle late.

Example: BANK HIRING CYCLE - 8 Weeks

| Bank requires new tellers (January) | Bank posts new teller openings (End of February) | Application deadline (Round 1) (April 10th) | Your resume submitted (Middle of April) | New tellers to start training (Beginning of May) |

Because you entered the Hiring Cycle for the bank teller position after the first application deadline, your chances for getting the interview, let alone the job, would have decreased drastically. The reason you didn't get the interview may not have been because you did not have the qualifications, but because they had already received a number of resumes and were satisfied in moving forward with those which they had received from the first round of applications.

Although in this example you missed the job opportunity, there are a couple of things you can do to correct this in the future. First of all, given that there is a Hiring Cycle inherent to every job opportunity, you need to be able to find out this information at the time you apply. This is probably the easiest piece of information to obtain from an employer. Here are some questions you can ask:

1. What is the application deadline for the position?
2. When do you plan to start to interview?
3. Do you plan on interviewing many individuals for the position?
4. What is the hiring process at your company?
5. What is the intended start date for the position?

These questions will enable you to find out information that will help you determine whether you have entered the Hiring Cycle at the right time. However, if you missed the application deadline but they are still accepting more resumes, you should always submit yours. The point I am making is that the more realistic you are about your chances, the easier it will be to maintain your motivation.

Earlier we talked about looking for employment as being a full-time job. It truly is a full-time job; each individual simply defines it differently. If the Hiring Cycle is an important factor when looking for employment, then we need to manage not only our time, but also the company's from whom we seek employment. This is not an easy task. Over the years, my clients have struggled with this notion. They became unmotivated in their job search activities because they did not feel in control of time. Anyone who tells you that you can control a company's hiring timeframe is simply wrong. I will not say that you can; what I'm going to tell you is that, although you cannot control the timing of the company's Hiring Cycle, you can control your own activity. What do I mean by activity? What I mean is your job search activity. Whether you are looking for employment on your own or working with an employment or career counsellor, you are the only one in control of your own time. If you are unable to manage your time during your job search and cannot get in line with the thousands of individual company Hiring Cycles (by the way, new ones are starting everyday), the likelihood of finding employment drastically diminishes. The goal during your job search then becomes to manage your activity. If the typical Hiring Cycle is eight weeks and you were to apply for a position today, you should, within eight weeks have a job (keeping in mind that you are the right person for the job). Now look at the same situation from the other side. If you do not apply for any job postings today, what is going to happen in eight weeks time? You already know the answer: you will not have a job eight weeks from today. You can see that your activity during the job search directly dictates your chances for employment success. If your job search is very active, and you are seeking out new opportunities for employment every day, your odds of success increase. If your activity is lacking, the chances for employment success decrease dramatically.

The Hiring Cycle is a funny thing. Over the years, some people have challenged this theory, claiming that if you are the right person for the job and you come late into the Hiring Cycle, you will be hired anyway. In some cases this can be true, but in most cases employers have already made up their minds. Again, it really depends on the type of position you are applying for and the company who is doing the hiring. For most jobs, the company who is hiring has a timeframe within which they have to work. Think about it: why do companies look for new people? One of the reasons could be that they have created a new position. This type of hiring may or may not be that time-sensitive, and so, with regard to the Hiring Cycle, it may not represent as important a factor as if somebody were to suddenly quit. The company may want to take their time and look for the right person. With most entry-level positions the reality is that the company needs to fill the position right away. Not tomorrow -- today! The Hiring Cycle in this example plays a pivotal role in the decision to hire. If you're not involved in the Hiring Cycle from the beginning, you definitely decrease your chances of securing the position.

Moving through the Hiring Cycle

If your activity is lacking, the chances for employment success decrease.

In the upcoming sections, we will discuss how to manage your activity and further understand the Job Search Process. Activity is critical to securing employment. In sales you often hear that the more prospects you are working on, the better the chance you have to sell something. I would tell my clients that if you go out day after day and conduct your job search, you're going to find a job opportunity by accident. Even if you were the most incompetent person on earth, if you conduct your job search on a regular basis, you're going to find a job. I am not saying that it will be your dream job, but you'll start to see what it takes to find "a" job, which is the key to the exercise. If you are in a position of presently conducting your job search (which I assume you are, if you're reading this book) you have to remember that this won't be the last time you go through this. That's why it is so important for you to understand the Job Search Process and the integral components that comprise it. You can't ignore them; you need to embrace them, which may seem overpowering and even sometimes frustrating. Putting your resume and cover letter together is important. Working on your interview skills is critical. However, these are truly only useful if they are being considered by the individuals who are doing the hiring.

Let's take an even closer look at the Hiring Cycle. By this I mean the time it takes a company to post a position and to fill it. Sounds simple! If we were to take, for example, a cashier position at the local hardware super center, what would their hiring process be? Even before we start to talk about the process, we need to think about why they would be hiring someone in the first place. The obvious reasons would be to replace someone who has either been promoted or who has left the organization. However, it could also be that they require more individuals, due to an increase in business, or perhaps they want to improve their ratio of cashiers to the number of customers who shop at the store. Whatever the reason, there are going to be different timeframes associated with each situation. Knowing this information would be valuable for someone who is interested in working at a Home Depot. Why they would want to know such information is something that many of my clients typically would not understand at first. However, after working with them, my clients would start to see how valuable this information actually was. The more information you have, the better the position you are in to understand the hiring philosophy of the organization. Knowing the Hiring Cycle is part of gathering information, which will move you closer to getting that dream job. With regard to the cashier position, most likely they would start by posting it internally, to see if any existing employees were interested in applying. Once they exhaust the internal options, they would then post the position externally. They might put it in the local newspaper, website, employment centre - anywhere they could get the most exposure. When they initially make the decision to hire someone, they look at when they want the new individual to begin. In most cases, especially retail, they try to stay as close as possible to the start date. The hiring manager is usually under a lot of pressure to get the right person for the job by a specific date. This is when the Hiring Cycle is mapped out. From the day they make the external posting until the day the new individual is supposed to start, represents the job seeker's window of opportunity for achieving employment success. That means the sooner you can become part of their Hiring Cycle, the better your chances of moving through their hiring process. If they have to fill the position within four (4) weeks, it means that manager is under pressure to fill the position within four (4) weeks. If you fill out an application or submit a resume in the third week of their Hiring Cycle that may mean that you have decreased your chances of getting the job.

How to enter the Hiring Cycle at the right time

It is one thing to know that there is a Hiring Cycle, as it comes to finding employment. However, the other side of the coin is knowing how to get involved at the start of the cycle. I want to let you know that there is no secret formula to knowing when a Hiring Cycle begins. Remember, Hiring Cycles are starting and ending every day. The key to getting in on the cycle at the beginning lies solely in your job search activity. The better we understand and manage our job search activity the more likely we are to get in at the beginning of the Hiring Cycle. As I mentioned previously, if you know your numbers, such as how many applications to fill out or how many resumes you have to submit to get an interview, the better your chances of entering a Hiring Cycle at the right time. If your ratio is 30 applications per week to five (5) interviews, then that means you have to find 30, 40 or maybe 50 opportunities to get those five (5) interviews.

How does the Hiring Cycle differ from industry to industry?

Depending on the industry in which you are trying to find a job, the Hiring Cycles differ in a number of ways. The first major difference is the supply and demand factor. If you are in an industry that has a shortage of workers, the Hiring Cycle is usually much shorter than an industry where there is an abundance of qualified people. The greater the demand by the employer for new people, the shorter the cycle will be as they will not want to take long to attract workers for fear of losing them to the competition. Consult your local employment center for information on labour trends for your industry in your area.

Another factor that affects the Hiring Cycle is the urgency of the employer to fill the position. If an employer has a huge hole in their workforce, the desire to fill the position as quickly as possible is critical. Finding out what this timeframe is and the urgency to fill a given position matters in two ways: First, if you are qualified you can express this fact that you would be able to start the position with little instruction. This, of course, is a huge benefit to the employer, as they not only require someone immediately, but someone who can come onboard and contribute right away. Second, you can offer up your immediate availability, if you are unemployed, since you do not have to give notice to an existing employer. Whatever the situation, it is important to identify what the employer actually is seeking. With some industries, Hiring Cycles are fairly lengthy and can require many interviews before a decision is made. In other industries, it may only take days.

Job Search Snack: **(JSS: 2-3) Specific industry Hiring Cycles (approximate)**

Industry	Hiring Cycle
Retail	As short as 2 weeks
High Tech	As long as 6 months
Hospitality	As short as 1 week
Professional	As long as 4 months
Agriculture	As short as 1 day
Medical	As long as 3 months

1. When should you enter the Hiring Cycle?

   _____

   _____

   _____

   _____

2. How can you determine a specific employer's Hiring Cycle? (Circle all that apply)

   a. Speak to the human resource department (if applicable)

   b. Speak to the specific department hiring

   c. Speak to an existing employee

   d. Look at industry standards

3. What is the Hiring Cycle for the type of job you are looking for?

   _____

   _____

   _____

   _____

   Answers can be found on pages 201-203. *

INGREDIENT 4

INGREDIENT #4: THE NEXT STEP

*(Deals with Job Search Forces **Reality and Motivation**)*

What's up?

I think it was that crazy rabbit that famously said, "What's up, doc?" I didn't realize what a compelling question that was until I started helping people find employment. The fundamental question that every individual who is presently conducting a job search must ask themselves is: "What's up?" It's important, as we work through our job search, that we have a good idea of what the next step is going to be. Let me give you an example. Many job search books on the market today promote the notion of following up whenever you go to an interview. Everyone knows how important it is to give the company who has just interviewed you a call or a letter thanking them for their time. Knowing what the next step is goes well beyond the simple process of following up with an interviewer. When I talk about knowing the next step, the underlying meaning behind this concept is the ability of the job seeker to become proactive about their job search. As I mentioned earlier in the book, you should at all times share control in the Hiring Cycle once you have entered it. I understand that in some instances this may be impossible. An interviewer may not wish to share with you some of the information that will generate the next step. What you must remember is that without a next step, you really have nothing. Furthermore, for a next step to occur, both the interviewer and interviewee have to be aware of what it is.

As was mentioned previously, the best opportunity for being successful during your job search is by moving step-by-step through the typical Hiring Cycle. This may seem obvious to you, but it is consistently overlooked. Time is also a factor in determining the next step. If the typical Hiring Cycle for an entry-level position is eight weeks, you need to be aware of this to optimize your chances for success. If you are going to remain "realistic" about a given job opportunity and you haven't yet heard from the employer in over four weeks, the likelihood of getting the job dramatically decreases. It becomes important to make sure that a job opportunity does not go beyond two weeks, unless the employer indicates that it has done so for a reason. **The goal in any job search is to remain as motivated as possible.** In light of this, your goal then is to eliminate all the job opportunities that are not going to work out. The reason you should do this is so that you can move on to another job opportunity that is more promising. This is more to keep your energy up and maintain a positive outlook during your job search. I've seen clients feel defeated because all of their hopes were put into one job opportunity. If you know what the next step is, whether negative or positive, you can act accordingly and have more control in the process.

What's the difference between following up and the "Next Step"?

Throughout my career I have worked with individuals who came back from an interview and said to me that it was probably the best interview they had ever been on. They felt that they were able to answer the interviewer's questions with ease and it appeared that there was a fit. My first question to them, after they filled me in with the details, was "OK, that sounds great. Now, tell me your next step." More often than not, especially with my new clients, the response would be something like this: "The interviewer said that they would get back to me in a couple of weeks with a decision, thanks for coming and have a great day!" On the surface this may seem like a next step, but if you examine it a bit closer, you start to see that it really isn't a next step at all. What could this individual have done to generate a next step? Let's dissect the interview process a little more closely. An interview has only two purposes: to determine for the company if the individual has the right skills and experience to perform the job and is the right "fit" for the organization, and for the candidate who is being interviewed to find out more information about the company and to see whether or not they have the skills to perform the job and if they want the job or not. This is the real reason for the interview process. Otherwise, the company would just accept the first person who called in and wanted the job. Keeping this in mind, the individual who is conducting a job search should not focus on one particular job. The accumulation of job opportunities is what is at the heart of a real job search. The notion of conducting a full-time job search is based on the principle of identifying as many opportunities as possible.

Let's examine the last point a little more closely. The Job Search Process does not involve the identification of one job prospect, but the accumulation of many employment opportunities. If this is true, and according to experience this has definitely been revealed to be the case, most individuals do not necessarily get the first job they apply for (unless they are extremely lucky). Rather, they work towards identifying a number of job opportunities in order to increase their likelihood of securing employment. So when I talk about the next step, what I essentially mean is that every time you go into an interview, you go in with a set agenda. The agenda may change from interview to interview, but the framework for the agenda is constant.

The Interview Agenda

Here is an example of an interview agenda. You have recently been informed that you have an interview set for the following week at 11:00 in the morning. You start to prepare for the interview by doing a background search on the company. You find out where they are located and determine how long it will take you to get there in order to ensure you will be on time. You start to formulate questions that you will ask the interviewer. How long have you been with this organization? What do you look for in a model employee? What is the long-term plan for the company? I used to refer to these types of questions as "fluff" questions in that they are not really providing any pertinent information which could be useful if it were at the

> *The notion of conducting a full-time job search is based on the principle of identifying as many opportunities as possible.*

beginning an interview time rather than at the end when you need to generate a next step. If you could ask these questions at the beginning of the interview then, based on how the interviewer replied, you could probably shape your own responses to their questions to you throughout the interview. However, in most cases the interviewer will unfortunately want to control the direction of the interview. Whatever questions you have for them, their responses to them are critical to determining the next step. Therefore, the agenda for the interview is another way of sharing control of the process. Depending on the company, the agenda will vary and change very quickly. The interviewer will try to set the tone for the meeting as they have a goal to find out as much information about you as possible.

In my experience, the interviewer's agenda is pretty standard: **to find out if the candidate is the right person for the job**. In an earlier section we spoke about minimizing the risk of the employer hiring you. The interviewer's job is to assess and determine the level of risk if they were to hire you.

What's on the Interview Agenda?

The interview agenda is actually quite simple. Although its content might change from time to time, the basic structure will always stay the same. The goal of the job seeker in any interview is to gather as much information as possible so that they can make an intelligent decision regarding working for an employer. You might think that it doesn't really matter what type of employer it is (especially if you need a job); however, if you are to manage the Job Search Forces it is critical that you approach each opportunity with as much control as the employer. Going through the Job Search Process is a state of mind. You are inevitably going to get rejected more often than you get accepted for the job opportunities that you identify. This is a fact of life and you need to be able to cope with it.

When putting together an Interview Agenda, five key agenda items are required. They are:

- Identifying the right person
- Ensure that you are being interviewed for the right position
- Identifying the hiring process
- Identifying the hiring timeframe

- Identifying the right income level

Identifying the right person: Before the interview is over, your goal is to determine whom the position reports to. In most cases it is usually the person who is conducting the interview. However, in more complex interview processes, the individual that the position reports to may not get involved until much later. Therefore, prior to leaving the interview, you must know whom you would be reporting to, if you were to get the job. In addition to finding out that the position reports to, it's important to determine who is involved in the hiring decision. This will ensure that you know to whom to direct certain questions throughout the interview process. By directing your questions accordingly, your opportunity for success will increase as you will then be able to better assess their responses and determine if your have a realistic opportunity of obtaining the job.

Sample Questions:

Would you be the person responsible for making the final hiring decision?

Will you be the individual this position will be reporting to?

Ensure that you are being interviewed for the right position: There are two aspects to this issue. First, you should make sure that the position you are being interviewed for is the one that you had originally applied for. This is important at the beginning of the interview because you will be directing your answers to questions based on the position you are interested in. I have worked with many clients who have gone on interviews only to find out halfway through that, in fact, what they thought they were being interviewed for was in fact a different position from that which they had originally applied for. Second, and most importantly, you should ensure that this is a position that you would want to do for 40 hours a week. In effect, is it what you had in mind? These types of questions are what you should have answered by the time you leave the interview.

Sample Questions:

Are there career advancement opportunities in this organization?

How would you describe the work environment?

Do you see me as a candidate that matches the position requirements?

Identifying the hiring process: How many interviews will you have to go on? How many people are involved in the decision making process? In larger organizations you may have an interview with the Human Resources department. If you meet the requirements at that level, they will then arrange a follow-up interview with the specific department doing the hiring for the position. Smaller organizations may only conduct one interview: with the decision maker. Whatever the size of the organization, it is important that you find out what the hiring process is to better prepare yourself for the next step.

Sample Questions:

If I'm successful, what is specifically involved in the hiring process?

Are there others involved in the hiring decision for this position?

How many interviews will there be for this position?

Identifying the hiring timeframe: The biggest de-motivator in the job search is waiting to hear back from an employer. This agenda item is more important than job seekers realize. You have to remember that you are conducting a job search and the timing of one opportunity may conflict with another one. Finding out when the employer plans on finalizing their decision on a candidate is critical. Also, you need to learn when the position will actually commence. These are all critical questions to your job search. If you are aware that the opportunity may not commence for a period of time, you are better informed to make a decision should another opportunity arise. In addition, from a psychological perspective, if you know when the decision will be made, you will not be "waiting by the phone" for their call and can thus continue to look for work.

Sample Questions:

When will the individual selected for this position start?

When do you plan on making the final decision for this position?

If I do not hear back from you, whom can I contact?

Identifying the right income level: Believe it or not I've had some clients accept jobs without knowing how much they were going to get paid. The sheer joy of getting a job overrode their need to find out how much they would be compensated. However, I must caution you on this. There are appropriate moments when this item should be brought up and it is usually best left to when the employer has offered you the job.

Sample Questions:

What is the salary range for this position?

How is the salary determined for the individual who is successful in getting the position?

I've determined through my job search that the range of salaries for a position like this is $0.00 to $0.00, where does this position fall?

When you come out from an interview and you can't respond to all of these items, this is a good indicator that you are not effectively sharing control. By having a pre-set agenda prior to an interview, the process will be much more relaxed and allow you to share control. In addition to your agenda, make sure to practice your interview techniques and seek the advice of either a professional or individuals you know who have just gone through a similar experience. When practicing for your interview, put together a list of questions that will help you identify the answers to the interview agenda items.

Do you always know your next step?

This is an important question. We've already spoken about understanding the job search odds and how important it is to maintain the necessary level of motivation. The same thing holds true for generating a next step. If you don't know what is going to happen next, how can you have any control over the process? You must understand that your job search efforts require you to gather information that allow you to identify what will happen next. The more you know, the better you will be able to understand your likelihood of getting the job. If you don't get the job, then you won't be surprised. After all, a job search is not easy work. It takes hard work, determination and, above all, the ability to take rejection. The next step will help you to determine whether or not you are progressing through the Hiring Cycle, or simply not moving at all.

Taste Test: (TT: 2-4) The Next Step

1. How is the "next step" different from following up?

    _____

    _____

    _____

    The purpose of the interview agenda is to *(circle all that apply)*:

    a. share control in the interview process

    b. take control of the interview process

    c. gather information

    d. generate the next step

2. What are the main items in the interview agenda?

    1._____

    2._____

    3._____

    4._____

    5._____

3. How will not knowing the next step affect your ability to successfully conduct a job search?

    _____

    _____

    *Answers can be found on pages 201-203. *

INGREDIENT #5: THE JOB SEARCH PROCESS

(Deals with Job Search Forces: **Reality, Activity and Motivation***)*

You have made it to the critical juncture in this book. This ingredient will illustrate for you the Job Search Process and the importance of moving from step to step within the normal job Hiring Cycle. The need to understand this process is pivotal to your job search success. When you think of the Job Search Process, you need to envision identifying an opportunity for securing employment in the exact same way as you would when planning a trip to the grocery store. Think about how you would go about it. You would: plan the list of which groceries you required; get in your car or onto the bus; park your vehicle; go into the store; search the aisles; proceed to the checkout; pay for your groceries; and then return back home. We continue to do it in this way, on a regular basis. We may even take for granted the way we go about buying groceries. It becomes just another thing that we do, even appearing at times to be an almost unconscious process. However, regardless of whether it's conscious or not, there is clearly an important step-by-step process involved. This is the same type of thing that you should expect to go through when looking for employment. Thus, the importance of what we put into what we need to do cannot be ignored, in order for it to become a regular routine and increase our chances for employment success.

What are the stages to the Job Search Process?

In almost everything we do in life, there seems to be a process that we go through. Whether it's assembling a new piece of furniture or getting married, we usually go through different

stages. The same holds true for finding a job. Think of the last time that you found employment (if this is the first time you're looking for a job, try and think of another example, like completing a school project or achieving a workout goal) and try to remember the steps that you went through to get the job. The first thing you probably did was to decide what if you wanted a job or looking for a new one. You then probably found out about a new job opportunity in the newspaper, online or through a friend. Once you decided you were interested in the opportunity, you put a resume together or went to the company and filled out an application. You then waited for a call from the employer and, on receiving one, attended an interview. Subsequently, you had to wait for a call to see whether or not you would get the job. Once you got the call and were offered the job, you were given a predetermined start date and then you actually started the job on this date. It's a pretty simple process, if you think about it. As we mentioned in an earlier section, the time it takes to go through such a process is typically eight (8) weeks. Your own particular experience may have taken more or less time, depending on what type of job you applied for and were offered. The point is that there are stages you go through when looking for employment. In fact, the importance of understanding each stage may play a fundamental role in achieving employment success within a shorter period of time.

If looking for work is a full-time job then where does one punch in? When working with clients, I would never discuss this aspect of the job search. To me it sounded almost de-motivating. You had to work full-time and not get paid! What was the point? I realized in the long run it would pay off, but we're not exactly living in a society that embraces the long-term.

Today, everyone wants things "now". If it doesn't happen by the end of the day, it's not really worth it. However, there is some truth to the old job search adage and it can be defined differently for everyone. Just because Jane spends 40 hours a week looking for employment doesn't necessarily mean that Bob has to spend the same amount of time without facing worse results. It does really depend on the person, what type of job they are looking for, where they live, and how many opportunities they can identify. What I provided my clients with was not merely a full-time job looking for work, but a useful framework that would provide feedback and help them monitor the Job Search Process. Some of my clients spent ten (10) hours a week looking for work while others spent much more time than that. It all depends on the level of activity of the individual and how quickly they wanted to find employment.

Enter the six (6) stages of the Job Search Process... Each stage contains both a unique experience and a requirement before moving to the next stage. The critical point here is that the best opportunity for employment success is in moving from step-to-step within the normal Hiring Cycle. The Hiring Cycle is dictated by the company to which you are applying (remember that you read earlier in the book ways of determining this). If you enter the Hiring Cycle either in the middle or at the end, the chance of getting the job is drastically reduced. Whenever I worked with clients and first introduced them to these stages, it seemed that was never particularly "earth -shattering" for them. As you will read, these are not complicated stages. Most likely they will make complete sense, at first glance. In other words, you could probably guess what they are. So before I present them to you, I would like you to write down

on the spaces provided below what you think they are. On the next page we'll start to specifically discuss what each stage is, and look at its importance.

1. _____

2. _____

3. _____

4. _____

5. _____

6. _____

STOP! Only turn the page when you have thought about the stages first.

In this part of the book we'll go through, in detail, the various elements of each stage. In Part three (3) of the book you will be provided with strategies on how to move through the job search stages in a timely manner. The six stages are:

1. Identifying Job Opportunities

2. Applying to the Job Opportunity

3. The setting of the Interview

4. Going to the Interview

5. Receiving the Job Offer

6. Starting the Job

STAGE ONE: Identifying Job Opportunities

The beginning stage! This stage should only commence once you have identified what type of job you want and are qualified to do. This could include a number of different types of job possibilities. At this stage you don't really need to have a cover letter or resume. Don't even worry about practicing your interview skills. The key in this stage is to analyze your social network and determine which contacts can provide you with job-related information. This is where you can determine whether you are in the flow or not. Getting in the flow is as important as writing your cover letter or resume. The contacts that you have or are going to make will provide you with the information you need to make you successful in finding a job. Although we will be talking about how your network can provide the type of information that can lead to employment, social networks represent much more than that. Many individuals who are in the process of looking for work find support from their networks in many different forms. This can include emotional, financial and/or motivational support. Our family, friends, neighbours, religious leaders and political figures are an important part of the job search journey. However, for the purpose of this book, we will be specifically looking at how our networks can potentially provide job-related information that can help us make the transition to the labour market.

How Do I Identify Job Opportunities?

This is probably one of the most difficult tasks you'll face during your job search. The more traditional method of looking for job leads in the newspaper is not going to cut it anymore. The majority of jobs that are available today are considered part of the hidden job market. That simply means if you don't know where to look for them, you won't be able to apply for the opportunities. What is the hidden job market? The hidden job market is basically located in that which you just completed a moment ago: your social network."). Your social network analysis is basically what will lead you to all those job opportunities. It may not be your primary contacts that will provide the job leads, but the secondary contacts who have a much farther reach than you. At the beginning of this section we spoke about knowing the numbers and came to the realization that you will have a much greater opportunity for success by increasing the number of contacts you have who can provide job-related information.

So how do you increase the number of contacts? The first step is already done: identifying your social network and the contacts within it. You now need to grow your network in order to get into the flow of job-related information. You can do this through a number of different vehicles. Adding contacts to your network can be accomplished via:

- Educational institutions

- Employment training programs

- Networking meetings (i.e. breakfast clubs)

- Taking a different route home

- Shopping malls

- Religious activities

- Government officials and departments

- Your children's activities (i.e. soccer team)

- Volunteer work

- Internet chatting and discussion groups

- Employer cold calling

- Employer information interviews

- Annual general meetings

- Libraries

- Museums

- Other social occasions

All of these examples represent opportunities to grow your network. If you're trying to grow your network, you have to get as creative as possible about meeting people. If you're shy, make connections through your existing primary contacts. Let as many people as you can know that you are looking for work. The more contacts you make, the greater the likelihood of coming across some job-related information that can help you find employment.

> ### *Job Search Snack:* (JSS: 2-4) What is the hidden job market?
>
> Simply put, the hidden job market equals the contacts you have in your social network. Therefore, if you have fewer contacts or are unaware of the information your contacts can provide, your access to job opportunities is limited. If you have a number of contacts with diverse backgrounds, access to the hidden job market is, as a result, much greater.

Getting in the flow of Job Related Information

Everyone belongs to a social network. Some networks are larger then others. However, all in all, networks provide a form of support. Whether it is financial or emotional support, we all tend to look to others for assistance. Getting in the flow of job related information is the concept of obtaining information from contacts beyond your traditional social network. What

I mean by this is that it is important for us to create contact relationships with other individuals **that we would not necessarily otherwise make**. Why should we do this? The main reason we should increase our number of contacts is that we might intercept a piece of information that is beneficial to our job search. For example, suppose that you typically don't speak to the individual behind the counter where you purchase your daily newspaper. Then, for no particular reason, one day you decide to introduce yourself. You realize it's silly not speaking to this gentleman; after all, you do see him almost everyday. Therefore, you introduce yourself and mention to him that you are in the process of looking for work. By coincidence, he had just been speaking with another customer the other day that works for a distribution company in need of warehouse workers. It might not be exactly what you want, but you do need a job and so you ask him for the contact's name and number. And, thus, you find you're the beneficiary of having been in the flow of job-related information in new ways that you were not previously.

The goal in any job search is to remain as motivated as possible.

This is just an example of what can happen when we "get into the flow" of information. It is human nature to stay within our own comfort zones. This includes the people that we converse with. Now, as an example, let's assume that your network consists of ten (10) people and that every individual in your network is also connected to ten (10) people. You can see now that we have about 100 people who may be able to provide job-related information. Your chances of getting into the flow definitely increases, if you are in contact with more people. It makes sense! However, this is easier said than done. Making new contacts on a regular basis may be more difficult for some people than others. Without the "gift of the gab" or the ability to start conversations with people we don't know, making contacts can be a threatening experience for some. You've probably noticed that some individuals have a natural knack for starting conversations with complete strangers, while others tend to shy away. In my experience, one of the biggest barriers to finding employment is the inability of people to make new connections. It is especially difficult for those individuals who have been unemployed for an extended period of time. The longer they've been unemployed, the smaller their social circles tend to become and the more difficult it is for them to make new contacts. This is an issue, which if not rectified, can hurt a person's chances not only of finding a job, but finding a job that specifically matches their goals.

How to "Get into the Flow"

We've already said that the longer you've been unemployed, the harder it is to make new contacts. We could say it's a lack of confidence that stops us from starting a conversation with someone we don't know. The bottom line is, however, that the more contacts we make, the greater our chances of getting into the flow of job-related information. After you read the rest of this paragraph, I want you to put the book down and close your eyes. Visualize yourself approaching an individual you have never met before. To make it easier for you, assume that the person you are approaching knows about a couple of job openings. All you need to do is simply go up and ask them about the opportunity. Now put the book down, close your eyes and visualize what you would say to this person in order to get this information out of them.

What did you say to the individual? How did you approach them? Did you introduce yourself? Did you tell them that you were looking for a job and you were wondering if they knew of any opportunities? Think of how excited you felt in the past, when you found out that someone you knew was aware of an employer who was hiring. Try to remember that feeling of excitement and your interest in getting as much information as you could out of that person. "Who's hiring?" "Are they still looking for people?" "Do you think I could get a job there?"

Now let's suppose you do not know the individual who has information regarding job opportunities, or are, in fact, unaware of whether said person may actually know of any job opportunities at all. Your conversation in the above scenario might have sounded something like this:

You: Hello, sir, my name is John, how are you today?

Person: Hello John, I'm doing well, thank you.

You: I was wondering if you would be able to help me?

Person: Well, that really depends on what kind of help you need.

You: Actually, I'm in the process of conducting a job search and I was wondering if you knew of any job opportunities?

Person: Hmm, let me think. I don't know of any myself, but I may be able to see if the company I work for is hiring in other departments.

You: That would be great. I would appreciate any leads you could provide me. Would you happen to have a business card, so I can follow up with you?

Person: Sure, no problem at all (hands you a business card).

You: Thanks for your help! I look forward to speaking with you again, soon.

The above conversation seemed to go pretty smoothly, didn't it? Even though that individual did not know directly of an opportunity, he seemed willing to see if anyone in the company he worked for was looking to hire. Of course, this was an imagined conversation. Things don't usually go quite that perfectly. But what would be the worse case scenario? Perhaps the person would say: "Go fly a kite! I don't want to talk to you!" **One thing that I've learned over the years is this: People are generally willing to help.**

I don't speak for everyone, but overall I truly believe that if you gave someone a chance, they would be willing to help you in some way. The key point here is "chance". In order for someone to help, they need to know whom they're helping, why they should help and in what way they can help. These critical factors need to be communicated in order for them to provide the type of assistance you require.

How we communicate is critical on **three levels** during the Job Search Process. The first level is simple: If we are unable to communicate to a potential employer during a job interview, then the chances of getting the job are drastically reduced. This is why we must practice our interview skills. The first impression or how we articulate our skills, background and experience is the most important skill a job searcher requires.

The second level, which may not appear as obvious as the first one, is how we approach people for job-related information. The easiest way to do this is to simply ask: "Are you hiring?" or "Do you know an employer who is looking for people?" Although these seem like two simple questions, they are not necessarily easy to carry out. Let's suppose that you asked those two questions at random to every second person you came in contact with. Depending on your present situation, you could come across a large number of individuals or, alternatively, you may not come across anyone if you were to stay in your home all day. If you were to ask everyone you met these questions, your responses would probably be somewhat negative. The approach you take to find out about employment opportunities is extremely important. As was noted earlier, some of us have a natural ability to communicate and to develop a rapport with individuals we have never met. For others, it is a little more difficult. The key to adapting your communication style and rapport is to first understand what you are trying to accomplish.

One thing that I've learned over the years is this: People are generally willing to help.

An Action Plan is essential when you are looking for work. This is not because it's going to tell us where we're heading, but because it will tell us where we've been. What I mean is that an Action Plan, although future-oriented in nature, is actually a historical instrument. Of course we develop Action Plans so that we can determine where we're going, but in most cases we rarely pick up the Action Plan after we've created it. What I like to do with my clients is to develop an Action Plan and then work through the scenarios, as if they have already taken place. What can we learn from this process? By following this approach we start to see "the reach" that is required to accomplish our employment goals. By reach, I mean the number of contacts we need to make in order to find the information that is required for a successful job search. You need to understand how interactions among the people you come in contact with on a regular basis is the most important aspect of your search. By understanding these dynamics, you'll start to adjust and adapt your Action Plan. Later in the book, we'll specifically look at communication and rapport building during your job search. As a result, you'll be able to open a conversation and ultimately get the type of information you require regarding your job search goals.

The final level regards how you communicate within your social network. The value of contacts is determined by the amount of job-related information your network can provide. To be in the flow of this information you need to be able to determine the appropriate level of interaction that is required to stay on top of new information. This is not always an easy task. First, there is a chance of annoying your network if you are always in contact with them. Although it is important to you that you stay on top of the information flowing in and out of your network, it is not necessarily the priority of other members. Keeping this in mind will help you strategize possible solutions for remaining optimally in the flow of information, while at the same time not upsetting your contacts.

It is important that you are aware that communication is your greatest ally when looking for work. Not all of us have the "gift of the gab" or the ability to go up to someone and ask for something. This is a skill that can be learned if it is part of your Action Plan and you are able to get assistance in this regard. In Section 2 (Identifying job opportunities/prospects) we'll get into more detail about utilizing your network.

What Employers Like

When conducting your job search you need to keep in mind that "employers" are people too. They think and react the same way as you and I. When it comes to hiring, they typically like to hire people who are like themselves. More importantly, they like to hire people to whom they or people that they know are linked. Many employers like to get referrals from existing employees. When a new position becomes available, the employer is most likely to go to their staff to see if they know anyone who would be interested in working at the organization. In order to get in touch with these potential job opportunities, you need to meet as many people as you can. The following pages will walk you through a network audit that will help identify who is in your network and if you need to add new contacts. Take your time and explore the contacts you already have in order to determine whether there are hidden job opportunities.

Primary vs. Secondary Contacts

What's the difference between a primary contact and a secondary contact? The simple answer is that a primary contact is an individual with whom you are in touch on a regular basis. Such contacts could be family members or good friends. Primary contacts are basically defined as those individuals whom you do not have a problem contacting and feel at ease asking for information or help. The potential problem with primary contacts is that they are typically linked to each other already and the information that flows between them is often redundant. Secondary contacts are those individuals that can be defined as acquaintances. You don't necessarily see them on a regular basis or you may only know them through another contact. The potential benefit of these contacts is that they are not necessarily closely linked and the chance for new information flowing into your network is much greater. It is important that you understand the differences between these two types of contacts, as each of them will have their own value in terms of providing job-related information. Again, the goal is to get in the flow of job-related information. Identifying the quality of information flowing into your network is important to know, so that if the information is not suitable to your job search you can start make new contacts who can help provide job leads.

Job Search Activity: (JSA: 2-4) Conducting your first social network Audit

The first thing you need to do is identify and write down the contacts in your network. At this point you only need to indicate your **primary contacts** – those individuals with whom you are in contact on a regular basis. The blank spaces will allow you to organize your list of contacts. If you require additional spaces, be sure to use a separate sheet.

Primary Contact List Form

Name	Position	Industry	Length of employment
_____	_____	_____	_____
_____	_____	_____	_____
_____	_____	_____	_____
_____	_____	_____	_____
_____	_____	_____	_____
_____	_____	_____	_____
_____	_____	_____	_____
_____	_____	_____	_____
_____	_____	_____	_____
_____	_____	_____	_____
_____	_____	_____	_____
_____	_____	_____	_____
_____	_____	_____	_____
_____	_____	_____	_____
_____	_____	_____	_____

Now that you have exhausted your list, we should categorize the contacts into different groups. Take your contacts that you have identified in your network and place them under the appropriate headings below. Note: Contacts can be under more than one heading.

Grouped Contact List Form

Employed	Provides Financial Support	Provides Emotional Support	Provides Child Care (if applicable)
_____	_____	_____	_____
_____	_____	_____	_____
_____	_____	_____	_____
_____	_____	_____	_____
_____	_____	_____	_____

_____   _____   _____   _____
_____   _____   _____   _____
_____   _____   _____   _____
_____   _____   _____   _____
_____   _____   _____   _____

_____   _____   _____   _____
_____   _____   _____   _____
_____   _____   _____   _____
_____   _____   _____   _____
_____   _____   _____   _____

The next step is to determine how far reaching your network is. This simply means how diverse your network is and how many other potential contacts you may have beyond those individuals you have listed above. An example of a low reach network and high reach network is illustrated below.

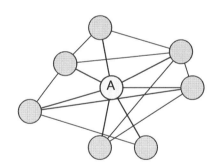

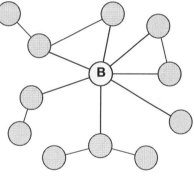

Low Reach Network   *High Reach Network*

Take a separate piece of paper and put yourself in the middle with a circle around your name. Draw a line away from your circle and put another circle with a name of the contact in it (Step 1). Keep adding lines from your circle with as many contacts as you have (Step 2). Once all your contacts are identified by circles and lines, you start to connect your contacts to each other (Step 3). In some cases there won't be any connection between contacts, in which case should not be any line indicated between them. Continue to make these connections through the use of lines until all your relationships and your contacts' relationships are indicated completely. Try and think of as many contacts as possible. Contacts can include, friends, former co-workers, classmates, neighbours, politicians, religious leaders, teachers, professors, lawyers, plumbers, etc.

Step 1 – Draw a circle with your name in the middle, and then connect a line to another circle with your first contact's name in the middle of it.

Step 2 – Continue to add lines and circles with other contacts.

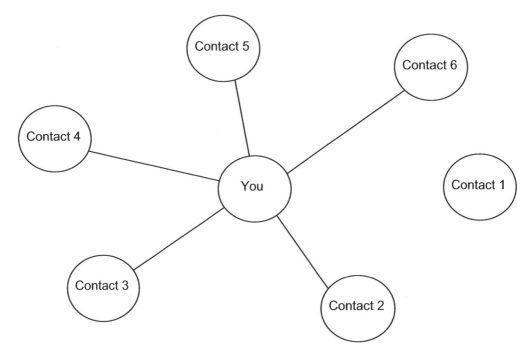

Step 3 – Start to connect your contacts with a line if they know each other. If the contacts don't know each other, there will be no line between their circles.

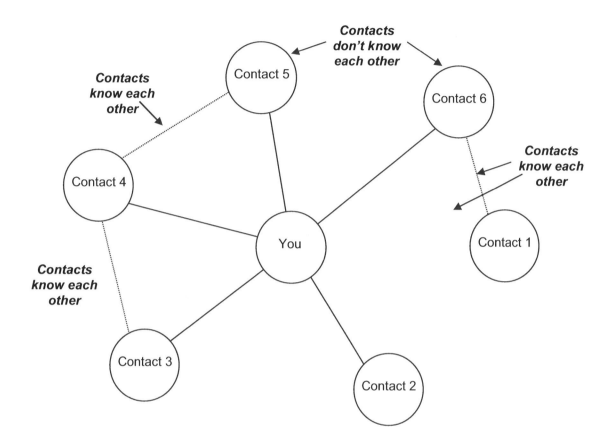

Now take your list of primary contacts and identify the contacts that *they* might have. We will refer to these individuals as **secondary contacts**. These contacts are those individuals whom you know only through your primary contacts. If you don't know their employment status, consult with your primary contact to gather this information.

Secondary Contact List Form

Name	Position	Industry	Length of employment
_____	_____	_____	_____
_____	_____	_____	_____
_____	_____	_____	_____
_____	_____	_____	_____
_____	_____	_____	_____
_____	_____	_____	_____
_____	_____	_____	_____
_____	_____	_____	_____
_____	_____	_____	_____
_____	_____	_____	_____
_____	_____	_____	_____
_____	_____	_____	_____
_____	_____	_____	_____
_____	_____	_____	_____
_____	_____	_____	_____
_____	_____	_____	_____

When you have listed as many secondary contacts as you can, take the chart from Step 3 (Second Contact List) and add the newly identified contacts.

Step 4 – Add all the secondary contacts to your primary individuals, which you have already plotted. Some of your primary contacts may have more than one individual they know.

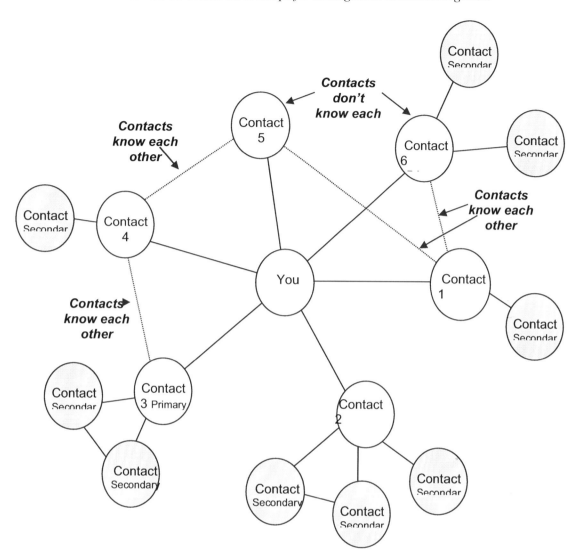

Now that you have graphed out your social network, the goal is to continue to analyze the contacts you have on a regular basis. As you strive to make more contacts, your network will continue to expand. Don't be discouraged if your network appears to be small at first. As is the case with most people, you've likely forgotten to put a few names down. It is important to keep this diagram handy so that as you remember or come to make new contacts, you can add them to your network!

Strategies for increasing the number of contacts in your network

Planning

Develop a SMART objective (specific, measurable, action-oriented, realistic, time-bound). Develop detailed strategies to achieve your objective. Ensure that you have an Action Plan A & B.

Research

Research various networking groups and associations to find out which ones will work for you. Research your contacts' information by asking them questions, so you will know whom you are dealing with. Research every possible opportunity. Keep your eyes and ears on the news, current events, and local developments as you may uncover information on hiring opportunities.

Self Promotion

Promote yourself effectively. Understand your features and benefits (your strengths and how to use them) and learn how to express them, as required.

Communications

Communicate effectively. Good communications are invaluable in any situation. Be articulate, concise, enthusiastic, honest, and open. Use language with which you are comfortable, but make sure it is powerful. Don't forget the other side of communicating -- listening. This is as important as speaking. Don't make the mistake that so many people do. Rather than listening, they spend their time thinking of the next thing they are going to say, thus taking in virtually nothing at all.

Think Creatively

Solve problems and maximize opportunities with innovative ideas. Rarely does an answer present itself in black and white. You have to assemble it, create it, and think it through.

Follow Through

Follow through on your commitments, both to yourself and others. A good referral or piece of advice only becomes activated into help when you follow it up.

Record Keeping

Take full and accurate notes. Otherwise, you will never remember what you've committed to do. Keep lists, schedules, and cross-referenced files. Write reminder notes about people you've met on the back of their business cards. Remember to keep your business cards in your right pocket and collected cards in your left pocket, so you don't give out someone else's card!

Organization

Organize yourself: your thoughts, your notes, your files, and your time. This may take you time in the short run, but it will ultimately save you time, in the long run.

Job Search Snack: **(JSS: 2-5) Online Social Network Audit**

You can go to http://www.socialnetworkaudit.com to complete an online network

audit and manage your contacts. This unique tool allows you to email your

friends and family, and encourage them to add their contacts to your own list.

Taste Test: (TT: 2-5) Identifying Job Opportunities

1. Where can you go to identify job opportunities?

    _____

    _____

    _____

    The best place to find a job from the list below is:

    a. Newspaper

    b. Internet

    c. Television

    d. Your network

2. Is it important to know whom your contacts know?

    True   False

3. Should you know what each of your contacts do in terms of their work?

    True   False

4. Do employers like to hire individuals referred by their own employees?

    True   False

5. What are some strategies to increase the number of contacts in your network, based on what you have read in this section?

    _____

    _____

    *Answers can be found on pages 201-203. *

Next Steps: Opportunities

- Conduct a network audit.

- Determine who your primary and secondary contacts are.

- Determine the type of job you are looking for.

- Develop Action Plans A & B.

- Develop a script to let people know you are looking for a job.

- Get help from a friend, family member, job coach or counsellor, if you require it.

STAGE TWO: Applying to the Job Opportunity

Letting the Employer Know You're Ready

Now that you have identified your job opportunities or, at the very least, put yourself in a position of being in the flow of job-related information, you need to start to apply to some of the job openings. Your goal in this stage is to take the opportunities you've identified in the first stage and move them to this one. Remember, once you have entered this stage, the clock starts to tick. Each of the employers to whom you apply has most likely established a time frame for when they want someone to start. This could range from a week to six months, depending on the position and industry. Once you have applied, you basically have two weeks to determine a next step. If this opportunity goes beyond the two-week period, the chances for getting the job decrease with each passing day. This is not to say that you don't have a

chance of getting the job after two weeks; I'm simply stating that the longer you do not hear from an employer, the more likely it is that they are not considering your application.

Before you apply, you should ensure that you have acquired as much information as you possibly can. If the odds of you getting this position are pretty good, the last thing you should do is apply right away. The first thing you should do is to try and get in touch with the employer to ask a few questions. If you're thinking that most of the opportunities state, "Please do not contact the employer directly" it may be an indication that most of your job leads are coming from the newspaper or online job boards. This means you are not accessing the hidden job market. Suppose, for illustrative purposes, that you are looking for a cashier's position in a large retail store. You found out about the opportunity through one of your secondary contacts. The deadline for the application is in the next couple of weeks, so you have some time before it is due. The most natural instinct would be for you to apply as quickly as possible. As soon as you apply, you have little recourse for asking questions and getting yourself to be a stand out among the many other candidates. Here's what would happen if you submitted your resume or filled out an application first, and then tried to gather information:

You: Hello, may I speak with John Smith? (The call is transferred). Hello John, it's Susan Dover, I was wondering if I could ask you a few questions about the cashier position?

John Smith: It would be best, Susan, to submit a resume along with an application form. I'll contact you if we're interested in giving you an interview.

You: Yes. In fact, I have done that.

John Smith: Great. So, as I said, we'll contact you if we're interested in giving you an interview.

You: Oh. Um, thank you.

Now let's suppose you haven't submitted a resume or completed an application form. The conversation could potentially sound something like this:

You: Hello, may I speak with John Smith? (The call is transferred). Hello John, it's Susan Dover, I was wondering if I could ask you a few questions about the cashier position?

John Smith: It would be best, Susan, to submit a resume along with an application form. I'll contact you if we're interested in giving you an interview.

You: Actually John, I plan on doing that, as I'm extremely interested in the position. However, before I do that, I want to make sure that this is the right position for me, so I don't waste your time. Do you mind if I ask you a few short questions first?

John Smith: Sure. What would you like to know?

You: What specific experience are you looking for?

John Smith: Well, you don't necessarily have to have retail experience as a cashier. Our system is quite unique and requires specific training you would not get anywhere else. Of course, the individual would have to be personable and be able to work effectively in busy circumstances.

You: Oh, that's interesting. So you're not looking for someone who necessarily has experience, but rather is personable. How do you determine if the individual is personable and that there is a good fit?

John Smith: Well, I look for individuals who have a wide range of experience, and I'm not just talking about work. I like to hire people who have volunteer experience and those who have been part of clubs in high school.

You: That's great. It looks like I have the types of skills you're looking for. I will definitely apply for the position. Again, my name is Susan Dover, and I look forward to participating in your hiring process.

John Smith: Thanks, Susan! I'll keep an eye out for your resume and application.

This conversation is much different than the first scenario. The key here is to separate yourself from the rest of the candidates. When the John Smith in our example looks through his resumes, he will probably remember this conversation not because he remembers your name, but because you will attach a cover letter to your application *reminding him* of your conversation. Whenever one of my clients would identify an opportunity that they were extremely interested in, I always encouraged them to contact the employer before they submitted their resume. Your goal is to increase the odds of getting an interview at this stage.

Getting in contact with the employer and gathering more information on the position will increase your chances.

Job Search Snack: (JSS: 2-6) Getting more information from the employer before you apply

The key to gathering information from an employer, who you know has already posted a new position, is to call them and ask if they have any positions available (do not call and tell them you know they are hiring and you just want to collect more information; they'll simply tell you to submit your resume). Even though you know they are hiring, you will be more successful if you approach it from the standpoint of conducting a job search and are inquiring to know if they have any opportunities within their organization.

Here are some questions you can ask, prior to submitting a resume or filling out an application:

If you speak with the decision maker directly:

- Do you anticipate a significant amount of interest in this position?

- Are you looking for candidates with a lot of experience in this field, or does it matter?

- What specific skills are you looking for?

- What type of educational background is required for this position?

- Before I submit my resume, I was wondering if you would consider hiring someone like me who does not have the specific experience you're looking for?

- To whom would this position be reporting?

- When do you plan on making your final decision for this position?

If you cannot speak with the decision maker:

- Is there more than one position available?

- To whom would this position be reporting?

- Do you also report directly to this individual?

- How long have you been with this organization?

- What skills do you believe are required for this position?

- Is experience an essential part of the selection criteria?

- Would you mind if I mentioned in my cover letter that I spoke with you about this position?

These are examples of the questions you could ask prior to submitting your resume. Remember, your goal is to gather as much information about the opportunity as possible so that you can customize your resume to meet the position's requirements. If you are not able to speak with the decision maker, speak with someone who works with them, so that you can refer to the conversation in your cover letter. Make sure that the individual you are speaking with has a direct relationship with the decision maker. If you want to increase the chances of moving the opportunity to the next stage, gather as much information as possible so you can increase your odds of getting an interview.

Determining what type of resume to submit

Now that you've identified a job opportunity, you need to determine which type of resume you will submit. It is extremely important that prior to submitting your resume that you determine the type of resume that is most appropriate. Before you send your resume, you must consider the following:

1. Do my skills, education, experience and background match the requirements of the job?
2. What are the odds of getting the position, based on my answer to the above question?
3. Is this job opportunity in line with my Action Plan (A & B)?
4. Has this job opportunity been referred to me? If so, how can I leverage the referral itself in

   order to increase my chances of getting the job?
5. Where did I identify the job opportunity (i.e. newspaper, friend, cold call)?
6. What information have I collected regarding this job opportunity that will help increase my

   chances?

The Targeted Resume

The targeted resume is dynamic in that it will always be changing. The information you gather about a specific job opportunity will help to develop your targeted resume. It is encouraged that you attempt to contact the employer prior to submitting a resume in hopes of gathering information for your resume. If it is not possible to contact the employer prior to submission, attempt to obtain information from other sources that will help to target your resume for the particular opportunity. More effort goes into the targeted resume than the generic one, and should be used for job opportunities that closely match your skills, abilities, background and experience. Evaluate the job search odds prior to submission.

Resume sample provided by Daisy Wright (www.daisywright.com)

Miriam Martinez
3914 Skyview Street
Toronto ON, M5M 3C5

Phone: **(H)** 905•777•0000 **(C)** 647•555•0000
Email: miriam.martinez@domain.com

JOB TARGET⇨ INDUSTRIAL ENGINEER
Increase Productivity… Reduce Operational Costs…Re-engineer Production Processes

An experienced and highly skilled industrial engineer with a solid background in analyzing processes through the use of engineering tools; methods and techniques which optimize product flow and streamline operations. Possess excellent multi-tasking, project management, problem-solving and cost-benefit analysis skills, strong customer interface capability, proven negotiating and sub-contracting skills. **Core expertise includes**:

Production Planning & Scheduling	**Productivity Improvement**
Materials Management	**Inventory Planning**
On-Time Delivery Improvement	**Training & Development**
QA/QC Programs & Systems	**QA/QC Performance Reports**
Advanced Knowledge of SAP/R3	**Proficiency in MS Office Suite**

EMPLOYMENT EXPERIENCE

Production Supervisor
E F G I N T E R N A T I O N A L , Toronto, ON   Dec 2007 – Present
(A leading provider of consumer products with a focus on convenient foods and beverages, and a workforce of 33,000 worldwide)

Hired as Quality Control Analyst, gaining entry back into my field of training, and within 4 months promoted to Production Supervisor. Collaborate with product development staff to design and implement quality control standards and procedures, initiated corrective measures where necessary, and monitored staff compliance.

Key Accomplishments:

Minimized lubrication waste by **50%** by using root cause analysis concepts to assess operational conditions of production lines and training **15** technical staff on equipment lubrication procedures.

Spearheaded the creation of **ISO 9000 Manuals,** which laid out detailed operating procedures designed to improve product quality and standards.

Increased efficiency by **20%** on **4** production lines by analyzing and implementing changes to machinery and equipment and optimizing production schedules based on demand.

Key member of the project team that implemented **SAP/R3 Production Planning Module**; Subsequently chosen to train **15** supervisors on the use of the system.

Converted assembly line to flow lines and redesigned flow line process to achieve a **5-day** product

Machine Operator
GHI CHROME PLATING, Brampton ON   Oct 2006 – Nov 2007
(Company chrome plated the molding surface of components used in plastic-injecting molds. These components were then used in the manufacture of plastic bottles by companies around the globe.)

Started as a volunteer to gain Canadian experience, but offered permanent position after eight weeks due to personal productivity, initiative and ability to be flexible during peak periods.

- Prepared and inspected parts prior to, and after application of chrome, and directed quality assurance program to ensure product quality was never compromised.

- Troubleshoot and corrected problems; monitored, identified and resolved quality problem areas, and prepared reports and documentation.

- Assisted with the design and manufacture of custom plating equipment, which had previously been outsourced.

Lead Engineer
JALISCO ENTERPRISE, Mexico   Aug 1998 – Jul 2006
(A subsidiary of La Fiesta Fine Foods of Italy with locations in Australia, Mexico, North America and United Kingdom)

Offered internship position upon graduation from University and through a series of promotions became the Lead Engineer for a 25-member production team.

Key Accomplishments:
- Reduced inventory cost by **40%** by developing production schedules and monitoring inventory levels of raw materials and finished products.

- Enhanced learning levels of over **60** supervisors and staff by developing and delivering an in-depth computer training program, which reduced data entry error by **60%** within **2** months.

- Collaborated with product development staff to design and implement quality control standards and procedures, initiated corrective measures where necessary, and monitored staff compliance.

- Extracted and analyzed data from SAP, generated key performance indicators' reports and presented same to senior management at meetings.

- Created efficiency graphs to analyze employees' performance and motivate them to improve productivity and meet deadlines.

EDUCATION & TRAINING

Casene Institute, Toronto ON
Production Planning Certificate (2009)
Universidad de Guadalaraja
BSc (Industrial Engineer)
Quadalaraja, Mexico (1998)

The Generic Resume

The generic resume is a standard resume that you can send out in bulk to many job opportunities. Sending out a generic resume reflects the assumption that your likelihood of getting the job is limited. It should be limited to one page and should only cover the most important aspects of your work history. The generic resume should be developed to make the employer want to find out more about you. If you do not get an interview you will not be as disappointed because you will have invested minimum time and will be aware of the odds of getting a call.

Resume sample provided by Daisy Wright (www.daisywright.com)

Job Search Snack: (JSS: 2-8) Example of a Generic Resume

Miriam Martinez
3914 Skyview Street
Toronto ON, M5M 3C5

Phone: **(H)** 905•777•0000 **(C)** 647•555•0000
Email: miriam.martinez@domain.com

INDUSTRIAL ENGINEER | PROJECT CONTROLLER | PRODUCTION ANALYST | PRODUCTION PLANNER

FUNCTIONAL EXPERTISE

- **Production Planning and Scheduling**
- **Productivity Improvement**
- **Materials Management**
- **Inventory Planning**
- **Manual Procedures**
- **On-Time Delivery Improvement**
- **Training & Development**
- **QA/QC Programs & Systems**
- **QA/QC Performance Reports**

SNAPSHOT OF QUALIFICATIONS

- Exhibit strong planning and scheduling skills, ensuring efficiency and productivity are not compromised.
- Skilled in bringing people and ideas together, building consensus and implementing solutions.
- Strong multi-tasking and time-management abilities; able to get the job done within tight deadlines.
- Proven effectiveness in working tactfully with managers, coworkers and vendors to boost productivity.
- Excellent communication, research, analytical and organizational skills.
- Fluent in **English** and **Spanish** with a very good command of **French** and **Italian**.
- **Bachelor of Industrial Engineering.**
- Proficient with **SAP/R3**, Word, Excel, PowerPoint

- Minimized lubrication waste by **50%** by using root cause analysis concepts to assess operational conditions of production lines and training **15** technical staff on equipment lubrication procedures.

- Spearheaded the creation of **ISO 9000 Manuals,** which laid out detailed operating procedures designed to improve product quality and standards.

- Increased efficiency by **20%** on **4** production lines by analyzing and implementing changes to machinery and equipment and optimizing production schedules based on demand.

- Key member of the project team that implemented **SAP/R3 Production Planning Module**; Subsequently chosen to train **15** supervisors on the use of the system.

- Reduced inventory cost by **40%** by developing production schedules and monitoring inventory levels of raw materials and finished products.

- Enhanced learning levels of over **60** supervisors and staff by developing and delivering an in-depth computer training program, which reduced data entry error by **60%** within **2** months.

- Collaborated with product development staff to design and implement quality control standards and procedures, initiated corrective measures where necessary, and monitored staff compliance.

- Extracted and analyzed data from SAP, generated key performance indicators' reports and presented same to senior management at meetings.

- Created efficiency graphs to analyze employees' performance and motivate them to improve productivity and meet deadlines.

EMPLOYMENT EXPERIENCE
EFG INTERNATIONAL, Toronto ON (Dec 2007-Present)
Joined as **Quality Control Analyst** and promoted within **4 months** to **Production Supervisor**

GHI CHROME PLATING, Brampton ON (Oct 2006- Nov 2007)
Machine Operator

JALISCO ENTERPRISE, Mexico (Aug 1998- Jul 2006)
(Fast-track Promotion)
Lead Engineer
Production Supervisor
Production Analyst
Coop Student

EDUCATION AND TRAINING
Casene Institute, Toronto ON
Production Planning Certificate (2009)

Universidad de Guadalaraja
BSc (Industrial Engineer)

The Cover letter template:

The cover letter template is produced to provide you with a sample that you can customize each time you send it to a job opportunity. The key to the cover letter is to tailor it to each specific employer for use with a targeted resume. If not, you can create a standardized cover letter to send along with your generic resume. Typically, you should include an opening paragraph indicating your interest in and fit with the organization, followed by your key accomplishments indicated in bullet point form. Conclude the cover letter with a closing paragraph indicating your interest in and fit for the specific job opportunity.

Job Search Snack: (JSS: 2-9) Example of a Cover Letter Template

Miriam Martinez
3914 Skyview Street
Toronto ON, M5M 3C5

Phone: **(H)** 905•777•0000 **(C)** 647•555•0000
Email: miriam.martinez@domain.com

October 12, 2012

Mr. Noel Belfonte
Director of Special Projects
NACO Chemicals
2465 NACO Drive
Markham, ON L3P 1X0

Dear Mr. Belfonte:

After carefully reviewing the requirements for the position of **Engineer – SAP Project**, I am submitting my résumé for your consideration as I believe I have the qualifications and experience to function very effectively in this role.

My several years of experience in production planning and inventory control, scheduling, and providing support in the development of new products are complemented by strong problem-solving and analytical skills. By investigating operational processes and implementing quality control procedures, I have been able to increase efficiency on production lines at EFG International by an average of 20%. This has had a significant impact on the profitability of the company.

I hold a Bachelor's degree in Industrial Engineering, a certificate in Production Planning, and was selected to be a member of the project team that implemented SAP/R3 Production Planning at EFG. I adapt quickly to new applications and technologies, and offer proficiency in MS Word, Excel and PowerPoint. In addition, my strong interpersonal and organizational skills and proven ability to do what it takes to get the job done have earned positive comments from peers and senior management.

After you have reviewed my résumé please give me a call at (905) 777-0000 if you have any questions. In the meantime, I look forward to meeting with you soon, and at that time we can discuss how my skills and background could add value to your production team.

Sincerely,
Miriam Martinez

Cover Letter sample provided by Daisy Wright (www.daisywright.com)

Submitting the Job Application

There are a number of things you can do when submitting an application that will increase the likelihood of you getting the job. It is important to follow the instructions on the application form exactly. The information requested by an employer is for the purpose of developing a profile of candidates and is used as a primary screening tool.

Tips for filling out a Job Application

1. **Try and get an application ahead of time** – If at all possible take the application form home, and fill it out there. The importance of filling it out accurately and completely is critical to ensuring that you make through the initial screening.

2. **Read all the directions first** – Make sure that you read the directions completely, prior to filling out the application. This will ensure that you include the information most relevant to the employer.

3. **Use N/A (not applicable) if certain sections do not apply to you** – This will demonstrate to the employer that you have read the directions. In other words, do not simply leave it blank.

4. **Do not write "See Resume"** – Make sure that you complete the entire application, as per the directions. Of course, you may consider attaching a resume to the application form, but make sure that you fill out the application in its entirety. Part of the hiring process for employers that request applications is to ensure that information is in one central location and can be looked at quickly. If you simply state, "See

Resume" it effectively means that you are not working within their process, and your application may be discarded.

5. **Make sure to use correct spelling and grammar** – Ensure that you are spelling correctly and using proper grammar. If not, this will reflect quite negatively on you and will likely hurt your chances of moving further along in the hiring process.

6. **Be honest** – Be honest when filling out the application. If you mislead the employer in any way, they will find out later in the hiring process.

Job Search Activity: (JSA: 2-4) Filling out the application

The key to filling out an application is to ensure that it is *fully and accurately* completed.

When an employer asks for an application to be filled it is usually part of their hiring process.

The following is an example of a completed application.

Sample Application

(Need to write in info)

Name (Type or print in ink)	Position for which you are applying: *Administrative Assistant*	☐ Full Time ☐ Part Time ☐ Temp	Date you can start: *Now*	Today's Date
Last *Doe* First *Jane* Middle Alexander				

Home Address		Home Phone: *(407) 555-1345*	Social Insurance No. *078-545-1129*
Street: *1345 Sesame Street*			
City: *Somewhere* State: *GA* Zip: *00055*			

Can be contacted now at:	Phone:	Have you ever applied for a position with us before? If yes, when? Position?
Residency Status Do you have the legal right to remain and to work in the Country? ☐ Yes ☐ No	Are you at least age 18? ☐ Yes ☐ No (Proof of age and work permits may be required before hiring).	Current/Last Salary: *$ 28,000/year* Salary Expected: $

Convictions:
Have you ever been convicted of a felony? (This information will be treated in a non-discriminatory manner.)   ☐ Yes   ☐ No
If yes, explain:

Answer only if applicable: Do you have a valid driver's license? ☐ Yes ☐ No	Has your driver's license ever been suspended or revoked? ☐ Yes ☐ No If yes, explain:

How did you hear about us? (or "this opportunity"): *From a friend in your department*

	Personal Computer/Model
	Software: Word Processing _____
	(WPM) _____ Spreadsheet _____
	Presentation _____ Other
	_____ Internet _____
	10-key Calculator? ☐ Yes ☐ No

Please complete the following sections even if the information is included on your resume:

Education	High School	College	Other
Name of School	*Sesame Street High*	*Honors College*	
Address	*Don't know*	*Don't know*	
Did you graduate? Yes/No	*Yes*	*Yes*	
Major	*High school courses*	*Public Relations*	
Minor	*NA*	*Spanish*	
Type of Degree/Grade Point Average	*3.8 GPA*	*Public Relations/3.4 GPA*	

Employment Record (Last 6 Years)

Are you presently employed? ☐ Yes ☐ No	Name of current or most recent employer: *Elmo and Associates*	Address:	Phone: *(407) 555-0123*
Type of Business: *Law Firm*	Name and Title of your Supervisor: *Mr. Smith, JD*		☐ Full Time ☐ Part Time ☐ Temp
Starting Date: Current/Final Date:	Starting Position: Current/Final Position:		Starting Salary: Current/Final Salary:
Describe your Principal Duties: *Calling clients; scheduling appointments for attorneys, note taking; all administrative office duties.*			
Specific Reasons for Leaving or pending leave: *Moved to another city*			

Over ⇒

Name of Employer Prior to Most Recent:	Address:		Phone
Type of Business:	Name and Title of your Supervisor:		☐ Full Time ☐ Part Time ☐ Temp
Starting Date: Final Date:	Starting Position: Final Position:	Starting Salary: Final Salary:	
Describe your Principal Duties:			
Specific Reasons for Leaving:			

Name of Employer Prior to Above:	Address:		Phone
Type of Business:	Name and Title of your Supervisor:		☐ Full Time ☐ Part Time ☐ Temp
Starting Date: Final Date:	Starting Position: Final Position:	Starting Salary: Final Salary:	
Describe your Principal Duties:			
Specific Reasons for Leaving:			

Other Significant Positions Held: (Name and location of company)	Supervisor	Phone #	Dates	Your Duties

May all of the employers be contacted for references? ☐ Yes ☐ No		
Include at least two more business references: Name	Relationship	Phone #

I acknowledge that I have been advised that this application will remain active only for the position applied for. I also understand that all offers of employment are conditioned on being able to supply satisfactory proof of an applicant's identity and legal authority to work in the United States.

Date: _____   Signature of Applicant: _____

Next Steps: Applied

- Contact the employer to find out about their hiring process.

- Find out when the deadline for applications is.

- Call the employer to find out if they have successfully received your resume or application.

- Get in contact with the interviewer, if you have been referred to them, in order to let them know that you have submitted your resume.

- If you have not received a reply to your application within one week of the application deadline, contact the employer to inquire.

STAGE THREE: Setting the Interview

Preparing for a Positive First Impression

You've identified the opportunity, and you've applied for the position. Now the employer has contacted you for an interview. It appears that you are in sync with the employer's Hiring Cycle. The date and time for the interview has been scheduled and you know with whom you will be speaking and have obtained details regarding the position. I'm sure you've read many job search books that cover such topics as interview techniques and negotiation skills, and it is important that you hone these skills. In addition to these skills, a positive first impression is one of the keys to increasing your chances of getting hired. If the interviewer likes what they see from the outset, your chances of getting the job dramatically increase. In my experience working with job seekers, the best way to ensure a good first impression is to be prepared for the interview. I also tell my clients that no matter what you do, you are not going to meet the expectations of every employer. This is something that needs to be understood before going to an interview. I've sent similar individuals to the same employer for an interview, and the one that I had thought had the better chance of getting the job, given their skills and experience, did not get it. This was not because they had a poor interview, or even said something wrong; the employer simply had a better connection with the other individual. As job seekers, we need to realize that the people interviewing us are human and have preferences for certain types of individuals. In other words, although they are employed by or own a business, they all have ideas of whom they want working for them. When you go on an interview do not make the mistake that you are interviewing for the company. In fact, you are really interviewing for an individual. If you use this way of thinking, it will help you to structure your interview, so that it will be focused and allow you to have some control over the process.

If you are speaking with the individual to whom the holder of the position reports during the interview, you need to find out how you can make their job easier than it is now. In most cases, the individual is looking for someone who can step into the position with minimal obstacles, and be up and going quickly. If you can demonstrate this to the interviewer, your chances of getting the job will dramatically increase. This is one variable of the process, but there can be a number of different variables that determine why an employer would select one candidate over another. The point is that the more information you gather, the better able you are to position yourself for the job.

Now that we've dealt with the issue of first impressions, hopefully, you can feel relieved of some of the pressure you might have previously felt about going to an interview. Let's discuss how we can prepare for a positive first impression.

The best way to ensure a positive first impression is to be prepared. Conducting your research about a company is the starting point, but it goes far beyond looking up information on the Internet about it. Preparing for an interview involves understanding the employer's Hiring

Cycle and the dynamics involved in going through that process. Remember that you are being interviewed by an "individual" and not a "corporation" or "company". The individual may represent the "company", but possess personal characteristics, and this must be understood if you are going to increase your chances of getting the job. For example, let's suppose that you have an upcoming interview at an insurance firm. The position is for an administrative assistant and it is scheduled to be held next week. What is the first thing you should to know about this opportunity? Most of you would probably answer that it is to gather standard information on the insurance firm itself: how long they've been in business, how many satellite offices they have, and the number of employees and the types of services they offer. This is all very important information and I encourage you to collect it, but will this information set you apart from the competition? In most cases you would not be the only candidate to be interviewed. If you were, you obviously would have been given a start date, not an interview date! The fact is that the employer will be interviewing a number of candidates with various backgrounds, skills and experience. The information you gather to prepare for the interview must assist you in being able to distinguish you from all of the other candidates being interviewed for the same position. The information or knowledge that you bring to the interview must demonstrate to the employer that there is minimal "risk" in hiring you. Simply put, if you can demonstrate to the employer that there is no risk in hiring you, the likelihood of getting the job dramatically increases.

Managing Risk as Part of Gathering Information

When an employer makes a hiring decision, it is usually based on the idea that the individual they've selected will fit nicely into their organization and will be able to perform the job at the highest level. The interview process allows the interviewer to determine the level of risk they would be undertaking in hiring a particular candidate. If the interviewer determines that a candidate may not fit into an organization, the candidate is labelled as "high risk" and most likely won't be hired. If a candidate is deemed "low risk", their chances of getting selected for the position are greater. This is not to say that each employer consciously assesses the risk factor associated with each candidate. It is almost an unconscious process and their goal in an interview is to determine which candidate (or candidates) fit into their organization and would, thus, represent the least amount of difficulty, in terms of being integrated into the position.

If employers are trying to limit the risk associated with hiring a new person for their company, how then can we, as job seekers, reduce that risk? On the following form you will be able to do a risk assessment on yourself. You can complete this exercise even if you do not have an interview scheduled. Moving forward, prior to every interview that you go on, conduct a risk assessment specific to the job opportunity. When completing the risk assessment you must be as honest as you can.

As you may recall from the Job Search Force "reality", it will not do you any good to misrepresent yourself during this process. For each of the headings, list the appropriate information. Your goal is to determine how you can minimize the risk for the employer. Accordingly, this will provide you with ammunition in your interview. The "**skills required for opportunity**" and "**experience required for opportunity**" and "**abilities required for opportunity**" will require some information gathering on your part.

__Job Search Snack:__ **(JSS: 2-10) The goal of finding a job**

The ability to achieve your goal of finding employment is quite dependent on your ability to effectively minimize risk for the employer. This can be accomplished through your resume and the interview itself. The resume introduces you on paper and indicates to the employer the relevancy of your background to the position. The interview validates your resume, and how you respond to the interviewer's questions determines the perceived risk. If you cannot minimize any perceived risks, your chances of landing the job are dramatically reduced.

Job Search Activity: (JSA: 2-5) Risk Assessment Form

Let's now go through the two examples above to see how you could use this assessment as part of your interview. However, before we go through the examples, let's discuss how you would go about collecting the information for the assessment. First of all, gathering this type of information is of great benefit. It will allow you to get in contact with the employer prior to the interview, and gives you an opportunity to collect information that will minimize the risk to the employer. The first example is for an administrative assistant and the second example is for a cashier at a grocery store.

Opportunity:						
Skills you possess	Skills required for Opportunity	Experience you possess	Experience required for Opportunity	Abilities you possess	Abilities required for opportunity	Additional attributes you possess
Example 1						
Computer Literate	Word Processing	2 years	3 years	Quick Learner	Must learn in-house system	Committed
Example 2						
Can operate a cash register	Working with a cash register	4 years	No experience	Problem solver	Deal with customer complaints	Customer focused

The ideal situation in preparing for the interview would be to find out a little more about the position so that you can determine how you are going to minimize the risk for the employer who will be considering your candidacy and, therefore, aid your chances of being selected.

The first thing you can do is contact the employer to see whether there is a job description for the position. If there is no job description available, this will give you an opportunity to speak with the employer further. The benefit of doing this is that you can gather information from the employer and use it to customize your resume. A typical information gathering conversation with the employer could sound something like this:

You: Could I speak with Mr. Smith, please?

Mr. Smith: This is Mr. Smith speaking.

You: Hello Mr. Smith. My name is Jane, and a friend of mine by the name of Betty Jacobs told me that there was an opportunity for an Administrative Assistant position within your department. Is this correct?

Mr. Smith: That is correct. We're looking for someone who'll be able to start right away.

You: That's great. I'm actually quite interested in applying for the position, but I wanted to make sure that before I do that I have the qualifications you are looking for. Is there a job description that you could forward to me?

Mr. Smith: We do have a job description for the position and I would be more than glad to forward it to you. Who did you say referred you to this opportunity?

You: Betty Jacobs from the Accounting department.

Mr. Smith: Oh Betty, that's great. I'll keep an eye out for your application.

If the employer doesn't have a job description, the conversation could possibly sound something like this:

You: Could I speak with Mr. Smith, please?

Mr. Smith: This is Mr. Smith speaking.

You: Hello Mr. Smith. My name is Jane, and a friend of mine by the name of Betty Jacobs told me that there was an opportunity for an Administrative Assistant position within your department. Is this correct?

Mr. Smith: This is correct. We're looking for someone who'll be able to start right away

You: That's great. I'm actually interested in applying for the position, but I wanted to make sure that before I do that I have the qualifications you are looking for. Is there a job description that you could forward to me?

Mr. Smith: Unfortunately, we don't have a written job description for this position.

You: Would you mind if I asked you some questions about the opportunity then?

Mr. Smith: No, not at all. What would you like to know?

You: What type of experience do you require for this position? What specific skill sets do you need? Etc.

You can see that calling the employer and asking for a job description provides you with an opportunity to gather information. As you become better at approaching employers, the quality of information you obtain will increase and, thus, the importance and relevance of it will be of greater value to your interview. The goal is to uncover as much information about the position and the individual who is doing the hiring. The easiest thing to do is to simply research what a company does. However, while this information is valuable and shows the employer that you were willing to take the time to investigate the company, it doesn't allow you to minimize your risk to them, as a potential candidate being considered for hire. Therefore, the value of information gathering regarding the position is a no-brainer.

Job Search Snack: (JSS: 2-11) Examples of Risks to employers

- Not enough experience

- Lack of specific skills/abilities

- Location

- Transportation

- Gaps in resume

- Personality

- Ethnicity

- Religion

- Attitude

- Work history

- Lack of education

- Over qualification

- Your overall presentation

Now that You Have Identified the Risk Factors, What's Next?

Now that you have identified the risk factors associated with the specific job opportunity, you are prepared to develop a plan of attack for your interview. In addition to the risk factors, you have also collected company information, the name of the person with whom you will be meeting, where the interview will be held, what you will wear, and how you are going to get there. These are all important factors when preparing for an interview, and they should not be overlooked. You can see, in looking to this list of information, that you have collected for this interview that you are prepared to conduct the interview itself. The goal for the interview is to feel as if you are in control and that the results of the interview will be equally by both you and the employer. Never forget that you have the option of *not* taking the job. I have found in my work with clients that "control" has always been a major barrier to being successful in a job search. Most individuals feel that the employer has total control, and although there is some truth to this, we have to remember that we are in the process of conducting a job search. When we are in the process of looking for work and it does not only include one employer. It usually involves a number of different opportunities. For each of these opportunities we need to determine which of them best fits our background, skills, experience, and, most importantly, whether we *want* to work with the organization. If you keep this in mind, hopefully it will relieve some of the pressure you feel when you go to an interview.

If you are working with a job coach or a counsellor, preparation for the interview is paramount and they will most likely suggest that you practice. Interview technique workshops and seminars are very helpful, and should be considered seriously. Interviewing is a skill and must be practiced on a regular basis, if you are going to become effective at it. The number of job changes you will face throughout your lifetime warrants investing time in honing this skill. When you start to go on interviews, remember that gathering information in advance is critical for increasing the likelihood of getting the job. By conducting a risk assessment, you will be effectively able to deal with any issues an employer may have about hiring you.

Taste Test: (TT: 2-7) Setting the interview

1. What would be a potential risk to an employer that is hiring for a night shift position in a factory?

    a. No college degree

    b. Limited experience

    c. No personal transportation

    d. All of the above

2. What are some of the risks *you* pose to a potential employer in your field?

    _____

    _____

    _____

3. What is your plan for minimizing those risks?

    _____

    _____

    _____

4. The key to finding a job is:

    a. Having a good resume and cover letter

    b. Memorizing appropriate questions to ask during the interview

    c. Making sure the employer knows how badly you want to work for their organization

    d. Minimizing the risk for the employer in hiring you

*Answers can be found on pages 201-203. *

Next Steps: Setting the Interview

- Make sure that you have conducted research on the company with which you are going to have an interview.

- Conduct a "risk assessment" for the specific job opportunity.

- Find out where the interview will be held, who will be the interviewer, and how you will get there.

- Practice your interview techniques.

- Discuss the upcoming interview with a job coach, counsellor, friend or family member, to get another opinion on your approach.

- Be prepared to explain what your skills are, as well as what you have done in the past.

STAGE FOUR: Going to the Interview

The Day of the Interview

It's the big day. The long hours you've put into preparing for the interview are about to be put to the test. You have practiced your interview techniques, and determined what your agenda is going to be. Everything is falling into place. If you do well at this interview you're almost guaranteed to get the job, or at the very least you feel you have a good chance of getting it. Prior to the interview, you have researched the company, so you're well aware of what they are all about. You know where they're located and you actually have the name of the person with whom you will be speaking. The interview is at 10:00am, so you decide to arrive a little early, but not too early...just enough to make some small talk with the secretary. You wait patiently in the lobby; you are a little nervous, but ready to go. The secretary tells you it's time and directs you to a room where the interview is to be held. You sit down and wait a few more minutes, before a gentleman comes in, introduces himself, and sits down. He asks you a couple of personal questions, and then tells you that he will be going through a set of questions that are asked of all candidates. So far, there is nothing out of the ordinary. You've been to interviews before and have found that they usually start this way. He goes through a number of standard questions like: *"Tell me about yourself"* and *"Why did you leave your last job?"* You've been practicing the answers to those questions, and so you breeze through them quite nicely. You're confident. He asks you a couple of scenario-based questions, such as:

"What have you done in this situation in the past?" or *"If you were confronted with this, what would you do?"* Again, this poses no problems; you've been practicing, and you have the answers. After a number of questions, he informs you that he has asked you all the questions he needs to, and is now wondering if you have any for him. You politely say thank you and start to ask the questions you had prepared prior to the interview:

"How long have you been with the company?"

"What do you look for in an employee?"

"How many positions are you hiring for?"

He answers all of your questions carefully, and you're satisfied with his responses. He tells you that he will be contacting you within a couple of days to let you know the next step. You say thank you and the interview is done.

Does this sound like a typical interview that you may have had in the past? What was the outcome? Did you get the job? Did you not get the job? In all likelihood, you went home after that interview feeling pretty proud of yourself. You answered all of the interviewer's questions thoughtfully and thoroughly. Your questions to the interviewer were intelligent and he spent a lot of time answering them. It almost felt like he enjoyed spending the time with you. All you had to do was to wait by the phone for him to give you a call, so he could let you know what was going to happen next. You figured he would call by the end of the following week. You were excited, but you knew you had some time to finish up some other things. The next week came along and you didn't get a call. You figured that he got busy and was unable to call you. After all, he did say in the interview that it was a busy time of year.

So you decided you would probably get a call, either the following Monday or Tuesday. Monday came along without a call being received. Tuesday arrived; again, there was no call received. It made you start to wonder. Maybe he was not going to call...because he expected *you* to give him a call. He might want to see if you had some initiative. You decided to give him a call on Wednesday. It was eight days since your interview. On Wednesday you gave his office a call, but all you could get was his voice mail. You didn't leave a message at first, because you were hoping to reach him in person. However, by the end of the day, after 20 failed attempts, you decided to leave him a message. The message you left probably went something like: *"Hi, my name is John, I had an interview with you last week and I was just following up with you to see what the next step is. If you could call me back at 526-555-5855 I would appreciate it. Thank you."* You told yourself again that he was probably busy throughout the day, and after listening to your message he would likely give you a call. Again, a couple of days passed and no phone call was received. You decided to try and call him again, and yet you continually got his voice mail. At this point, it was now twelve days since your interview, and you still didn't know what was happening. You made one last attempt at trying to reach him, and you were finally successful. He apologized for not getting back to you, but he had been extremely busy. He said that although you were a strong candidate, the company unfortunately had gone with another candidate who had stronger skills than you. You thanked him for the opportunity, hung up the phone, and proceeded to feel very disappointed.

I'm sure this exact scenario has happened to all of us at one time or another. We go to an interview thinking that we've aced it only to find out that we didn't get the job. This is the time when an individual's motivation to continue to look for work is facing its greatest challenge. Many of my clients have gone through this and it doesn't necessarily get any easier every time they do.

What if there was a way to minimize the blow? What if you were able to create an interview agenda and then actually stick with it? The **Interview Stage** is one of the most important stages of the Job Search Process. You have a fifty percent chance of getting the job and a fifty percent chance of not getting it. As was mentioned before, you can have as much control over the Job Search Process as the employer. In some cases, employers have a standard set of questions that they ask all candidates. This usually occurs in an organization that has a structured Human Resources department. However, in some organizations, the types of questions asked depend on the candidate being interviewed. Remember, it's not the company you've applied to that is conducting the interview...it's a **person** who is doing the interview. Those who conduct the interviews have personalities that are as wide and varied as the job seekers themselves. Moving to the next step is the goal of any interview. Whether it is another interview or getting the job itself, the sole purpose of the interview, from the job seeker's perspective, is to move forward through the Hiring Cycle.

Answering the Interview Questions

Prior to this stage (i.e. setting the interview) you have undoubtedly prepared for the questions that will be presented to you during your interview. The key to answering questions is to prepare prior to the interview. Seek the help of a friend, family member or job search professional to practice answering questions.

Job Search Snack: (JSS: 2-12) Sample interview questions (employer)

- What are your long-range goals and objectives?

- What are your short-range goals and objectives?

- How do you plan to achieve your career goals?

- What are the most important rewards you expect in your career?

- Why did you choose the career for which you are preparing?

- What are your strengths/weaknesses/interests?

- How do you think a friend or professor who knows you well would describe you?

- What motivates you to put forth your greatest effort? Describe a situation in which you did so.

- In what ways have your college experiences prepared you for a career?

- Why are you interested in this position?

- Describe your experience(s) working in a similar situation as this one.

- What have you achieved that has given you the most satisfaction?

- Describe your style as a team player?

- What kind of people do you prefer to work with?

- What have you learned from each of your past jobs?

Signs an Interview is Going Well – Listening for the Queues

The above example of an interview is a common indicator of what starts out seeming to be a sign of a good interview underway to a situation of not getting the job. Too often, I have seen clients come back to me and say that they had the interview of their life and yet not get the job. As a professional, I have become fairly effective at determining an individual's chance of getting the job after an interview. The number one mistake that people make when they go on interviews is that they memorize a bunch of questions that they plan to ask the interviewer, in hopes of demonstrating to the employer that they are interested in the position. Imagine that you wanted something from someone and that individual had the option of giving it to anyone they wanted. What would you do to get it? The last thing that I think you would do is ask them a bunch of questions that, most likely, everyone else was going to ask. You would probably try to convince the individual to give it to you and explain to them why only you deserved it. You would sell them on the idea that it should only go to you. Why should this be any different in an interview? When you're working within your interview agenda (see: **What's on an Interview Agenda**), you have the opportunity to present yourself as if you are determining whether or not you should work with them.

The easiest way to tell if your interview is going well is by the type of questions the interviewer is asking. In most interviews, the employer will usually start out by making statements in more general terms. For example: *"The candidate for this position will require the ability to be flexible"* or *"The candidate should be prepared to start within the next two weeks"*. If an interview is going well and the employer appears to be interested in the candidate, those general statements will be specifically directed to the individual. For example: *"I can see you working well in our department"* or *"You would be required to work closely with most of the departments in the organization".* You can see how the employer's language has changed and is more directed towards the candidate that they are interviewing. These are common cues, which job seekers often overlook. Whenever one of my clients came back from an interview, I would ask them if they identified any such cues during the interview process.

In addition, the goal of any interview you go on is to gather as much information as possible in order to determine your potential for getting the job. As was mentioned previously, your interview agenda should include gathering information that lets you know: if this is the right position; what the hiring process and the timeframe is; and if it is the right salary (see interview agenda for more details).

Your Turn to Ask Questions

You sat in front of the employer answering their questions and now it's your turn. We've already spoken about the interview agenda, and so this will help you guide the type of questions you will ask. Having your own agenda will ensure you collect the information you require to make your decision, as to whether you want to work with this organization or not. Remember, you're in the middle of a job search; you need to gather as much information as possible, so you can make the right decision.

Develop an interview agenda so that you can determine what information you require to help

you to determine whether you would like to work with this company or not. Your ability to

---

Taste Test: (TT: 2-8) Going to the interview

    1.   Develop your own personal interview agenda.

_____

_____

_____

_____

_____

_____

    2.   What are some signs an interview is going well?

_____

_____

_____

    3.   What information should you collect by the end of an interview?

_____

_____

_____

       *Answers can be found on pages 201-203. *

successfully reduce the risk to the employer hiring you can be achieved by virtue of how you present yourself. Having a reason for asking particular questions lends itself to an increase in your credibility, and, therefore, reduces the risk to the employer considering your candidacy.

__Job Search Snack:__ **(JSS: 2-13) Sample Interview Questions You Can Ask the Employer**

- How long have you (i.e. the interviewer) been working with this organization?

- What do you like about the organization?

- What are you looking for in an employee?

- How long have you been looking to fill this position?

- Why is this position available?

- What are the opportunities for advancement in the organization?

- What is the hiring process at your organization?

- Who will be making the decision regarding the position?

- When does this position start?

- At which location should this position be based?

Next Steps: Interview

- Make sure you know when the position will start.

- What is the follow-up process for the position?

- How will you contact the interviewer?

- Is another interview required?

- Are there any outstanding issues that you did not address in the interview?

- What were the risk factors for this employer?

- Have you reduced the risk for the employer?

STAGE FIVE: Receiving the Job Offer

The Job Offer

Congratulations! You've made it this far, but the journey is far from over. Depending on what type of job you have been looking for, the job offer is an important part of your job search journey. **The key here is to remember that, in the Job Search Process, once you receive a job offer, it is important to remain as calm and level headed as you can.** Remember that you have been involved in an extensive job search, which has involved a number of different potential employers. What a job offer effectively represents, is that you have been able to narrow down your list of employer candidates. The shared control that you have been experiencing throughout this process has shifted directly onto you. The level of control may be as simple as either taking the job or not, but the point here is that you have a very important decision to make. If you decide to take the job, it takes you out of the job market. If you don't take the position, you will continue to look for work. The key here is to take the information you have gathered in the interview to assist you in making a decision.

Before you make your final decision, you will be required to enter the negotiation phase. Whether it is negotiating for salary or for the shifts that you will work, now is the time to lay it on the line. In most cases, if the interview process has gone well there shouldn't be many surprises. Along the way you have gathered information that has allowed you to decide if this was the right opportunity for you. All you have to do now is cross the "t's" and dot the "i's", right? Whenever you are in a situation of receiving a verbal job offer, you should make sure that all of your bases are covered. For example, the starting salary is a critical factor because it will dictate all future increases. You need to know how the employer's review process works in order to determine your ideal starting point. Notice how I've focused on the review process. It's a lot easier to discuss with an employer how often they review employee performance versus asking how often each employee is eligible for a raise. Whether you are asking your local grocer or a Fortune 500 company, this will come across as an intelligent approach and reflect favourably on you. Basically, you're using the performance review as a way to find out about salary increases. The following Job Search Snack presents examples of how to find out more information about the employer and how they deal with employee issues:

Job Search Snack: **(JSS: 2-14) Asking indirect questions to get the answers you really want**

Indirect Questions	**What your really wanted to ask**
How often do you review an employee's performance?	When will I be able to get a raise?
How does the scheduling of shifts work?	Do I have to work weekends?
As an employee, what am I eligible for?	Do I get benefits?
How flexible is the work schedule?	Can I work from home?
How are vacation days accrued?	How many vacation days do I get?
How are employees encouraged to support the organization?	Do I get employee discounts?

Job Search Activity: (JSS: 2-6) Configuring your negotiation questions

Try writing a few questions that you would like to ask, but are unsure whether or not are appropriate. Work with someone to determine how you can reword your questions to best provide you with the answer you are looking for. **Tip: Write the questions you really want answered first, and then reword them in the "Indirect Questions" column so that they are appropriate.**

Indirect Questions	What you really wanted to ask

The key to this stage of the Job Search Process is to make sure that you have all your facts in order. You need to understand what you're getting into by asking the appropriate questions. Do not be rushed into making a decision. The best thing you can do is take the information from the employer and get back to them after you have thought the offer through. Tell the employer that you are excited about this opportunity but, because you are in the middle of a job search, you have to tie up a few loose ends before you make your final decision. This may at first seem presumptuous, but keep in mind the control factor. If you do decide to take some time, remember to be reasonable in terms of the amount of time you take. The last thing you should do, after all, is come across as not taking the offer seriously.

***Taste Test:* (TT: 2-9) Receiving the job offer**

1. What indirect question could you ask if you wanted to find out how much the position paid?

_____

_____

_____

_____

_____

2. Right down an indirect question to find out if you are being seriously considered for the position?

_____

_____

_____

*Answers can be found on pages 201-203. *

Next Steps: Interview

- Where will you be working?

- When is the start date?

- What is your salary/wage?

- How many vacation days are you eligible for? After how long a period of time will they increase?

- What is your work schedule?

- When are the performance reviews? How often are they conducted?

- Who will you report to?

- What opportunities are there for promotion?

197

Stage Six: Starting the Job

Let the Job Begin

Congratulations! You've actually started your job with a new employer. This is an exciting time and a momentary end to the Job Search Process. The reason I say "momentary" is that you never know when you will be making your next move. Now that you are employed it becomes much easier to look for a new job. Employers like to hire individuals who are already working. However, keep in mind that your new employer also can let go any employee at any given time. Obviously, finding a balance in your new relationship is important here.

If we follow the typical Hiring Cycle for an entry-level position, this journey will have taken a minimum of eight weeks. Depending on your background, education and work experience, it may have taken longer, or possibly, gone much faster. The key here is that reaching the "job stage" involves many different variables; some of these you can control, but for others there is nothing you can do. If you follow the suggestions outlined in this book you will be able to structure your job search in such a way as to allow you to identify what you are doing well and what needs improvement.

The First Day on the Job

You've finally accomplished what you set out to do when you started your job search. However, there are a number of things you must consider prior to your first day of work.

Most likely your new employer will orient you to the organization and your position. Specific training will be provided depending on your new role and a schedule will be developed to determine the length and timing of your orientation. Your first day on the job is a critical time for both you and your new employer. The following are some things you should consider:

Get Some Rest

You may consider taking some time off prior to starting your new job. If you've just recently completed school, you might be already well rested. However, if you're coming off another job, consider taking a week of vacation, so you can recharge your batteries.

Dress for Success

If you're required to wear a uniform for you new job, getting dressed properly for your first day will be quite simple. However, if you're not required to wear a uniform, think back to your interview and wear what you observed the individual's wearing at that time. If you cannot remember, drop by the organization prior to the start date, and observe what the employees are wearing. If you're still not sure, you can call your new boss and ask him or her what is appropriate.

Sample Questions:

What would be appropriate dress for my first day on the job?

What do you suggest I wear the first day?

Arrive Early

Arriving early shouldn't be a problem, as you most likely weren't able to sleep much the night before. However, this is extremely important so you should make sure that you know exactly where and how you're going to get to your new job. Set your alarm early enough to give you the time you'll need to get ready. Have a friend or family member call you in the morning, just in case. This is not a day you should be late. However, you ought not to be too early.

Make sure people know who you are

Not everyone is going to know who you are on your first day. That is why it's important to make every possible effort to introduce yourself. Your boss or supervisor may introduce you to key people, but not everyone. The best thing you can do is to offer a handshake, explaining who you are to as many people as you can. This may feel awkward, but it's essential in making a good impression with your new co-workers. All you need to do is say a few words like: "Hi, my name is John. I've just started here. How are you?" Also, when you have introduced yourself, try and remember people's names. If you're not good at remembering names, come up with a system that will allow you to do so. Name association works well for most people. For example, the name Fred could be more easily recalled if associated with the cartoon Flintstones. Also, because you're new, you won't be considered rude if you ask an individual to repeat their name to you. If anything, use the fact that you are new as an excuse for people to help you out.

Assess the Corporate Culture

Spend some time assessing the corporate culture of your new work environment. Consider coming in early to see what time people typically show up. Is it early, right on time, or are most late? Do the same thing in the afternoon to see how late people stay after their shift is over. This will help you to determine how things are done in this particular organization. You may also consider observing the following:

- How do co-workers prefer to communicate? (i.e. email, voice mail, or in person)

- How are certain individuals addressed? (e.g. Are supervisors referred to by first name or surname?)

- What is the dress code, and is it enforced?

- When and how long do people typically go for lunch and breaks?

Identify opinion leaders

Try and identify those individuals who are sought after by co-workers for company information, gossip, or leadership. Typically these individuals are not necessarily bosses or supervisors, but individuals looked upon as sources of information by fellow co-workers. Information provided by opinion leaders may not always be accurate, so you should be cautious.

Identify key players

Determine who the key players in the organization are (i.e. those who are looked to as critical to the company's success). Identify the specific skills they possess, and use this as a benchmark for monitoring your own progress. Try to develop a relationship with these top performers, so that you can gain from their experience and be viewed in a positive light from management. However, be careful how you do this, so as to not upset other co-workers that may see you as trying to gain favour from certain individuals.

Find out what your new employer expects of you

Make sure to meet early on with your boss to discuss specifically what they expect of you. This is important to your success within the organization. Ensure that you are directing your attention to what they feel is important at a given time. Do not assume that what you feel is important is the same thing as what your boss thinks is important. Some questions to ask your boss regarding clear expectations could include:

- What are the immediate priorities and issues that need to be addressed?
- How often would you like to discuss the relevant issues for my position and the organization?
- How will my performance be evaluated?
- Who is involved in determining the priorities for our department/organization?

Seek help from co-workers but be careful

Ask co-workers for their ideas and/or suggestions, but be careful. If you ask someone for his or her advice and you don't use it, there may be repercussions. The last thing you would want to do is upset someone early on. Make sure you communicate to your new co-workers that you're a team player and are willing to contribute like anyone else. When asking for help, make sure you ask in such a way as to permit you to reject (in a nice way) their suggestions. Here are a couple of examples regarding how you can do this:

Sample questions:

I was wondering if you could tell me how you would take care of this situation?

I'm new here and I'm gathering some ideas on how to take care of this situation, and was wondering if you could share your experiences?

Remain Neutral

Even if your department requires improvements and you happen to know the answers, do not offer advice unless asked. You need to develop some credibility prior to offering input that may dramatically change the way your new department functions. Do not use phrases, such as: *"We used to do it this way at my last job"* or *"You might consider doing it this way"*. The last thing you would want to do is alienate yourself from co-workers, by suggesting things too early on in your new employment.

Be Flexible

Expect the unexpected. Do not think that you can go into a situation and make changes right away. You want to make sure that you can "flow" in your new environment and, by doing so, come to learn how things get done. Whenever expectations are set for you by your boss that seem unrealistic, try not to react immediately. Instead, determine if they truly are unrealistic. If you still think your boss' demands are not reasonable, ask for clarification. Things will change from day to day; keep this in mind, and you should be able to make it through quite easily.

Remember what to do if you're on Plan B

If the job you're starting is based on Plan B, remember what you will need to do to get to Plan A. The reason why you took this job in the first place was to:

- Gain experience
- Develop new skills
- Access new contacts
- Engage the possibility of future promotion
- Get a paycheck!

I'm sure you can think of a number of other reasons but, most importantly, you need to remember how this new job can ultimately move you closer to your ideal job. The reason you originally created a Plan A and B, was with this very purpose in mind.

Taste Test: (TT: 2-10) Let the job begin

1. On your first day of work you should do the following (check all that apply):

   a. Introduce yourself to as many people as you can

   b. Suggest new ways for running the department

   c. Identify the opinion leaders

   d. Establish job expectations with your boss

2. What are some of things that you need to consider, when you first start your new job?

   _____

   _____

   _____

3. It is important to identify key players in the organization, so that you can determine what is considered to be an above-average performance for employees?

          True   False

4. When seeking advice from co-workers, you need to be careful not to upset anyone in case you do not use what they suggest. Provide an example of the kind of question that would not put you in a position to be obliged to take their advice?

   _____

   _____

   _____

   Answers can be found on pages 201-203. *

Next Steps: Starting the Job

- Get comfortable with your new surroundings

- Try and introduce yourself to as many people as possible, so that you can increase your network

- Make sure that you become familiar with your new organization's culture

- Learn the company's policies and procedures

- Show enthusiasm and a genuine interest in learning

- Remain flexible

PART THREE: A STEP-BY-STEP METHOD FOR IMPLEMENTING THE JOB SEARCH INGREDIENTS

Putting the Job Search Ingredients together

Focus on opportunities that have the greatest opportunity for success.

Now that you know what goes into the Job Search Recipe, it's time to start preparing the dish. We've attempted to illustrate the Job Search Process and the importance of moving from step-to-step within the normal Hiring Cycle (JS Ingredient #3). The need to develop an approach that is in keeping with the specific industry, in which you are looking for work, is critical to your employment success. Following the Job Search Process, as outlined on the following pages, will allow you to identify specific issues that are affecting your ability to move towards your job goals. In addition, by applying the principles identified throughout the book thus far, you will be able to structure your job search, so that you will be able to maintain your motivation. The Job Search Process is not an easy one, but with the framework provided here, you should be able to conduct a job search that will allow you to find employment in a timely manner.

Now that you have walked through the various job search stages, you've probably noticed that they are not especially unusual. Most of my clients are not surprised by the stages. The challenge is in moving from stage to stage within the normal Hiring Cycle. Through the use of a Job Search Board (e.g. on a piece of paper or a computer spreadsheet), you will be able to see your progress throughout each of the stages. For each job opportunity, you should move it through each stage within a certain amount of time. The reason for this is that you must be in sync with the Hiring Cycle timeframe. If you're not moving from stage to stage within the Hiring Cycle timeframe, the likelihood of getting the job dramatically decreases. What you need to do is to determine the most appropriate length of time a job opportunity can stay in any one given stage. The type of job you are looking for will dictate the length of time. So for example, if you selected two weeks, the opportunity has to move forward at the end of that period. In some cases it may remain where it is (e.g. you have found out that the hiring decision has been delayed). You will be able to determine this only if you can identify a "next step". If you can't identify the "next step" then move the job opportunity back to the first stage (Opportunity). It doesn't mean that there is no longer a chance of getting that particular job; it simply means that you don't have a next step. In part one (1) we spoke about the three Job Search Forces: motivation, activity and being realistic. If you don't have a next step, how can you truly be realistic about that particular job opportunity? Over the years, I've seen my best-qualified clients lose their motivation because they would hang onto a job opportunity

Job Search Snack: (JSS: 3-1) Determining the amount of time a Job Opportunity Card can stay in a column.

Examples by sector are provided. Keep in mind that the amount of time allotted a job opportunity, in terms of how long it should stay in a given column, should be for the sole purpose of encouraging a next step. In some cases, the job opportunity can stay longer than the designated time, if circumstances permit. For example, if you have a job opportunity as a Chef in the Interview column for longer than one (1) week because you have found out that the hiring decision has been delayed, the card can stay. This idea here is so that you can maintain a realistic outlook on your job search, and avoid getting overly focused on one job opportunity.

that they thought they would get, but never even received a phone call. You should avoid this at all costs and focus on opportunities that have the greatest opportunity for success.

* In the last row, enter your personal information, including: the sector in which you are looking for work, and the amount of time a job opportunity card can stay in a column.

Sector	Hiring Cycle (H.C.)	Reason	Time in Column (H.C. divided by 6)
Information Technology	4 weeks	Longer decisions made by employer to fill positions	
Hospitality	1 week	Large turnover	
Manufacturing	2 weeks	Quick decision making	
Professional positions	8-10 weeks	Lengthy hiring process	
Agriculture	6 weeks	Seasonal	
Government	3-5 months	Long hiring process	
Education	3-4 Months	The nature of the school year and a stringent hiring process	
Retail	3 weeks	Large Turnover	
*	*	*	*

<u>*Job Search Snack:*</u> (JSS:3-2) Reviewing the Job Search Ingredients

Ingredient #1 – Job search numbers: a number that serves as a guide to indicate how you're doing in your job search.

Ingredient #2 – The what, where, when, who and why of the job search: focusing on what you're doing during the job search, so that you can determine if your approach is helping you to find employment.

Ingredient #3 – The Hiring Cycle: The time it takes an employer to fill a posted position. This varies to from industry to industry and position to position. Where you live and the type of job you are looking for are factors in determining the length of the Hiring Cycle.

Ingredient #4 – The next step: generating the next step ensures that you are moving through the Job Search Process. As you attempt to move from stage to stage, ensure that you know what happens next. If you don't, you need to find out what will happen next. Knowing the next step will also help you to maintain both your motivation and a realistic outlook respecting your job search chances (see *Job Search Forces*).

Ingredient #5 – The Job Search Process: The Job Search Process is comprised of the stages. Each stage represents an opportunity to improve your chances of finding a particular job. If you are unable to move from one stage to another, you may require the help of a job

Gathering the Job Search Utensils

Now that you have the right ingredients, you now need to gather the necessary utensils that are required to start the Job Search Process. The following is a list of what you will require:

1. Targeted resume (See example JSS: 2-6)

2. Generic resume (See example JSS: 2-7)

3. Cover letter template (See example JSS: 2-8)

4. Action Plans for Job A & B (See example JSS: 1-2)

5. Job Search Board (See below)

The Job Search Board

This is a tool that will assist you in monitoring your job search progress. The Job Search Board has six columns: Opportunity, Applied, Set Interview, Interview, Job Offer and Job. Each column represents a unique stage in your job search efforts and allows you to monitor your progress each step of the way. The Job Search Board can be created with a notebook, by simply using a computer spreadsheet or going to www.snagpad.com for an online version. Unlike other job search approaches, the Job Search Board goes beyond the conceptual and provides a solid framework for the job search. The benefit of using the Job Search Board is twofold. The first use is in how you will now be able to monitor your progress to determine how well you are doing and moving through the Hiring Cycles. Second, you will be able to share your progress with someone who may be able to provide useful suggestions toward moving you along through the Job Search Process.

In order to get going using the Job Search Board, you are going to require access to a computer spread sheet, a notebook or an account on www.snagpad.com. If you are using a computer spreadsheet, you are going to type in your job opportunities and cut and paste them to a new column whenever it is time to move the opportunity to the next stage. If you have decided to use a piece of paper, make sure to use a pencil, so that you can erase a job opportunity from one column whenever you put it in the next. If you have created an account on www.snagpad.com, you will be able to convert job opportunities into job cards and manage them on a virtual job search board. Regardless of whether it is a computer spreadsheet, a piece of paper or www.snagpad.com, the set up is as follows:

Opportunity	Applied	Set Interview	Interview	Job Offer	Job

For each job opportunity, you are required to fill out as much information about the lead as possible. As you move the opportunity through the job search stages, you will be adding more information. The information you should focus on includes:

- Company name

- Position

- Job Description

- Contact Name

- Date opportunity was identified

- Date resume was submitted

- Interview date

- Next steps

- Contact Phone/Fax/Email

- Where the lead came from

- To Whom the position reports

Each time you identify an opportunity (lead, referral, and candidate) or apply for a position, set up a Job Opportunity Card with the following information:

1. Company Name

2. Date Applied

3. Contact Name

4. Next Step

- Each time you review your Job Search Board, ask yourself the following questions:

- Do I have enough employers on my board?

- Are the columns properly balanced? If not, what needs to be done?

- Am I being honest with myself?

- Does my Job Search Board tell a story?

- What has been done in the last two weeks?

You will notice in each of the columns that the titles are in their past tense voice except for the first one (i.e. the Opportunities column). The reason for this is that when you move a job opportunity to a column, it will be something that will have already occurred. The first column is the place where you store all of your potential job leads that have not yet been acted on. As soon as you decide to apply, the Job Search Process begins for that particular job opportunity. You can only move your job opportunity card to a given column if it meets its particular column's requirement, as listed below:

1. A job opportunity in the "**Applied**" column means that you have already submitted your resume or filled out an application.

2. A job opportunity in the "**Set Interview**" column means that you have an interview set, but you have not yet attended it.

3. A job opportunity in the "**Interview**" column means that you have gone to the interview.

4. A job opportunity in the "**Job Offer**" column means that you have received a job offer from an employer.

5. A job opportunity in the "**Job**" column means that you have actually started a job.

The Job Search Board represents a visual representation of the Job Search Process. By following the above rules, you will be able to quickly assess your progress in your job search. In addition, if you are working with a job search professional, they will be able to quickly determine how you are doing in your job search.

Get Cooking: Tracking your Job Search Activity

Now that you have gathered all the job search utensils, you can start the Job Search Process. The following pages will walk you through each of the columns in your quest for securing employment.

Job Search Board: First Step – Opportunity

Refer to Job Search Ingredient #1 and #5 for tips and suggestions

If you have decided to use a computer spreadsheet, apply the same principles and label six columns with the appropriate headings. Place every job opportunity on a "Job Opportunity Card", which basically is a card that contains all the information for a given job opportunity. As you move the "Job Opportunity-Card" through the stages, more information will be added to it. When you first identify a job opportunity, you should write the name of the company or organization in the **Company** field. If you know the **Contact Name** or **Phone/Fax/Email**, indicate them as well. Even a job opportunity has to have a next step, so under the **Next Step** field indicate when you plan on applying for the position. Will it be in a couple of days or weeks? Do you have to speak with someone before applying, so that you can gather more information in order to customize your resume? Do you need to find out the contact name? All of these questions should be asked prior to submitting a resume.

From now on, instead of merely writing a job opportunity down on a piece of scrap paper, you will be able to monitor all of your job leads and keep them organized. In addition to keeping track of your job leads, you also should keep track of your job search numbers (Part 2). These numbers should correspond to your Job Search Board. If you are just starting out and are identifying job opportunities, you should be recording one number; the number of job opportunities you are identifying (P). Of course these opportunities come from a number of various sources (e.g., newspaper, online job boards, friends and family).

Example Stage One: Opportunity

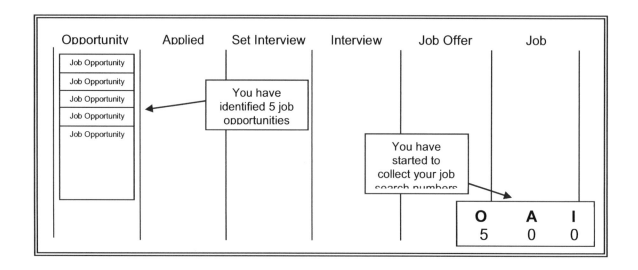

Job Stage Approach: Strategies for Moving my "Job Opportunity-Card" to the Next Stage

Reason for Job Opportunity Card in this Column: Opportunity

- No *next step* or you require more information prior to submitting your resume

- You need to attempt to contact the employer first

- Decision to hire has been delayed

- Gathering employer information (research)

- Creating a targeted resume is required

- Unknown application deadline

Ranking Questions

- There is no next step

- No decision is expected in two weeks

- Require more information

Questions to ask in order to increase the number of job opportunities in this column

- What other companies are similar to the ones I have been applying to?

- What are some similar companies, to those that have I worked for in the past, which I can approach for a job?

- Are any of my friends presently working and, if so, for whom are they working?

- If there is an application deadline, can I meet it?

- Do I need to speak with someone at the company to gather more information, so I can customize my resume?

- Who in my social network can I approach for job leads?

- Where else can I look for job opportunities?

- Is everyone in my social network aware that I am looking for work?

- Who can I seek help from, respecting job leads?

Overall Job Board Management

- What are the next job opportunities I should pursue and why?

- Who do I know that can refer me to a job?

Job Search Board: Second Step – Applied

Refer to Job Search Ingredient #5 for tips and suggestions

Once you start to identify job opportunities, the next step is to apply for them. Prior to submitting a resume or filling out an application, always try and gather as much information about the position as possible. You can customize your resume, if you have collected the right information about the position. Once you have submitted your resume, determine the odds of getting the job based on what we discussed in Part 1. Now that you have moved a job opportunity to the **Applied** stage you need to make sure that you have a *next step*. Determine the length of time that a job opportunity card can stay in this column. The length of time will depend on: the type of job you're looking for, its location (urban or rural), and your knowledge of the Hiring Cycle. Once this length of time has expired, you must either move the given opportunity to the next stage or go back. An example of a next step could be that you will contact the employer to find out if you are going to get an interview.

Example Stage Two

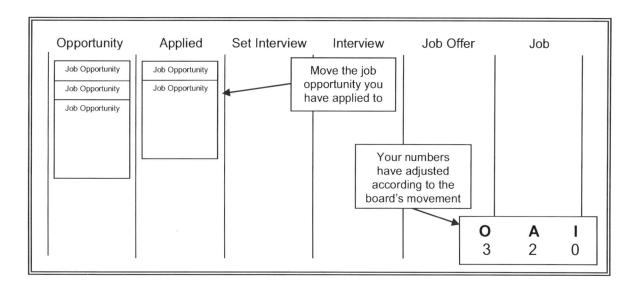

Job Stage Approach: Strategies for Moving my "Job Opportunity Card" to the Next Stage

Reason for Job Opportunity in this Column (Applied)

- Submitted a resume

- Filled out an application

- Waiting for an employer to call to arrange an interview

Ranking Questions

- What position am I applying for?

- When is the application deadline?

- What is my next step?

Questions to ask in order to increase the number of job opportunities in this column

- To whom am I submitting my resume/application and why?

- What do I know about the position I am applying for?

- Are there specific job requirements, and do I meet them?

- Where is the company located?

- How was the position advertised?

- Who will be conducting the interviews?

- Was I referred to this job opening by someone else?

- Was I able to contact the employer prior to submitting an application?

- Do I know anyone who works or has worked at this company?

Overall Board Management

- How many applications should I maintain at all times?

- What is the overall movement of this stage (i.e. "Applied" column)?

- Are there many job opportunities that don't go beyond this stage?

Job Search Board: Third Step – Set Interview

Refer to Job Search Ingredient #4 and #5 for tips and suggestions

You can move the "Opportunity Card" to the third stage (i.e. Set Interview) when you have received confirmation of an interview. This is a date that is set in the future and one that gives you time to prepare for the interview (see Section 2: Stage 3). Your next step for this job opportunity would be the date, time, and location of the interview. The two-week rule for this stage is flexible, although I have dealt with clients who had received calls for interviews that never actually came to be. You should make sure that if this does happen, you find out the reasons why, and whether or not it can be rescheduled.

Example Stage Three

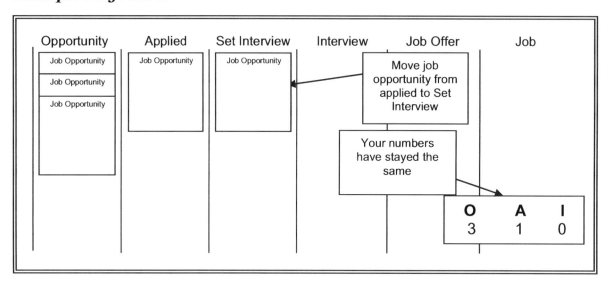

<u>**Job Stage Approach: Strategies for Moving my "Job Opportunity-Card" to the**</u>

<u>**Next Stage**</u>

Reason for Job Opportunity in this Column (Set Interview)

- An interview is scheduled with a set date and time

Ranking Questions

- What position is the interview for?

- Has the meeting been set?

- Where will the interview be held?

- Who will be conducting the interview?

- What is my next step?

Questions to ask in order to increase the number of job opportunities in this column

- Why are you interviewing for this position?

- What information have I gathered on the company?

- Have I determined my interview agenda?

- Have I prepared for the interview?

- Have I gathered the necessary resources?

- Will there be any formal testing involved?

- How will I respond to questions regarding experience or qualification gaps?

- What will I wear to the interview?

- How will I get to the interview?

- How early should I arrive?

- Where is the interview?

Overall Board Management

- What preparation has been made for the interview?

- How are my interviews scheduled?

- Do I have any control over when my interviews are scheduled?

- What type of companies am I typically getting interviews for?

- Where are these job opportunities coming from?

Job Search Board: Fourth Step – Interview

Refer to Job Search Ingredient #4 and #5 for tips and suggestions

At this stage you have already gone on an interview. It is important that you have identified the right person, right process, determined if it's the right position and timeframe, and whether or not it is the right salary. After each interview sit down and review what has been said in order to determine what your next step is. Each interview should serve as an opportunity to further develop your skills. If you're working with a job search professional you should debrief with them and develop a plan for future interviews.

Example Stage Four

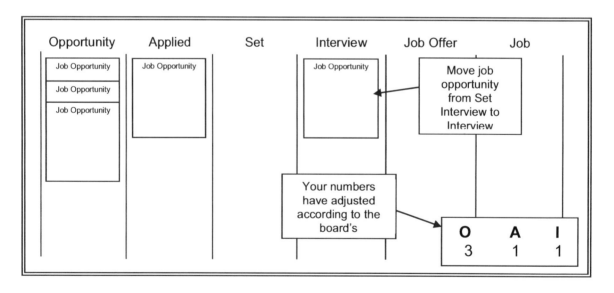

Job Stage Approach: Strategies for Moving my "Job Opportunity-Card" to the Next Stage

Reason for Job Opportunity in this Column (Interview)

- Attended interview

- Determined:

    o This is the right position

    o The right location

    o The interview process

    o The timeframe

    o The right pay

Ranking Questions

- Find out about the position, location, timeframe, process and pay

- Have you sent a thank you letter?

- What is your next step?

Questions to ask when a job opportunity is in this column

- When will the employer make their decision?

- What is the work schedule?

- Did I arrive early enough to give myself some time to prepare for the interview?

- Who will contact me with a decision?

- How many other candidates are competing for this position?

- How do my skills match the job requirements?

- Was I interviewed by the person to whom I would be reporting (i.e. if I got the job)?

- Is there more than one interview?

- How did I feel about the interview?

- What is my next step?

Overall Board Management

- What does this stage tell me about my recent job search activity? A low number may indicate:

    o I haven't applied to as many opportunities in the last two (2) weeks as I should have.

    o The poor quality of companies to which I have applied, in terms of those that do not go through a formal hiring process.

    o The recent positions for which I have applied do not match my experience and skills

    o Are there any employers in this stage that have been on your job search board too long and may have expired?

Job Search Board: Fifth Step – Job Offer

Refer to Job Search Ingredient #5 for tips and suggestions

This is an exciting stage. You've completed the interviews, you have generated the next steps, and now the employer has finally contacted you to offer you the position. However, although you are pretty excited about the prospect of working again, you still need to generate a next step. The most important thing is to find out the conditions and to negotiate an appropriate employment package. Again, you must not let excitement consume your focus; you must remember that you are still in the midst of a job search. There are other opportunities that you have identified, and you need to seriously take the time to determine which is the right opportunity for you. You should find out: the start date; if you will be working shifts or regular hours; where you will be working; who you will be reporting to; and how much you will get paid. At this stage, if you're working with a professional, you should discuss in detail how to handle the situation.

Example Stage Five

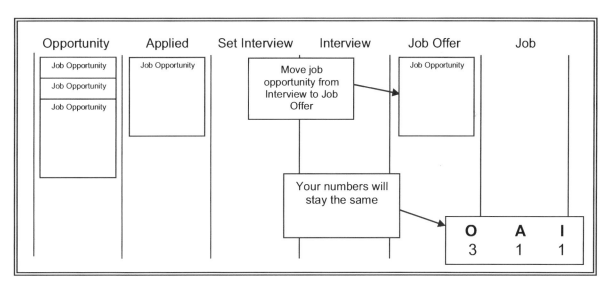

Job Stage Approach: Strategies for Moving my "Job Opportunity-Card" to the Next Stage

Reason for Job Opportunity in this Column (Job Offer)

- Verbal Job Offer

Ranking Questions

- When does this job start?

- I require a definite start date

- What is my next step?

Questions to ask in order to increase the number of job offers in this column

- When do they require a response?

- What will be my salary/wage?

- Does the company know I am presently conducting a job search?

- What is the start date?

- What is the work schedule?

- Who will I be reporting to?

- Where will I be working from?

Overall Board Management

- Have I followed up with the employer?

- Is any employer listed at this stage been on the job board too long?

- Do I have a 90% chance of starting this job?

__Job Search Board: Sixth Step – Job__

__Refer to Job Search Ingredient #5 for tips and suggestions__

Congratulations! Stage six is the final stage - at least for now. You've actually started the job, met your new co-workers and you know when you're getting paid. Yet, who knows how many times you may end up changing jobs or even, possibly, your career? You may even go through this process for promotions you have identified along your career path with the same employer. It is important to reflect on the journey that you have just gone through. Determine what worked well and what didn't work well, so that if you have to go through it again, you can reduce the time it takes to find a job.

Example Stage Six

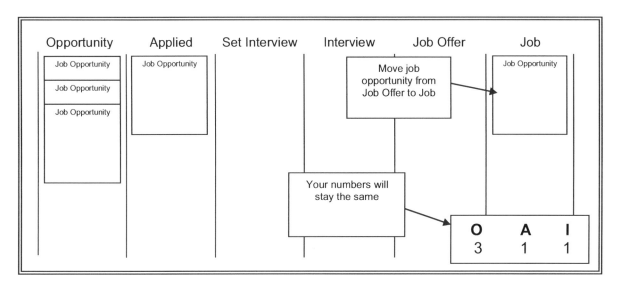

<u>Job Stage Approach: Strategies for Moving my "Job Opportunity-Card" to the</u>
<u>Next Stage</u>

Reason for Job Opportunity in this Column (Job)

- I actually started the job and am on their payroll!

PART FOUR: LET STAND 5 MINUTES, AND SERVE

Challenges of making the Job Search Management Recipe

Like starting anything new, it is often awkward and sometimes difficult to get into the groove. When starting out with the Job Search Management Recipe, you will require discipline due to the simple fact that following the practices in this book will not yet be second nature to you. The key here is to understand the Job Search Forces themselves, and how they affect your ability to move through the Job Search Process. Once you are able to deal with the factors that affect your ability to move forward, you likelihood for succeeding will dramatically increase.

The biggest challenge for job seekers is in identifying job leads. Your first instinct is to go to the newspaper and Internet. Although you can find qualified leads from these resources, keep in mind that other job seekers will be looking in the same place. If you're playing the job search odds, the odds are quite low of getting a job using these resources. That's not to say that you shouldn't search the newspaper, but you should be aware of what you're up against. Try and think outside the box and look for job search leads where you wouldn't typically try. How about a government official, or your local religious leader? Each of these individuals are part of a community and have connections. The key to identifying job leads is getting in the flow of information, and the best way to do that is to make contacts with people you would not typically approach. This may be an uncomfortable activity, but with practice you will start to become more comfortable. Remember that you're in the middle of a job search and it is okay to ask people if they know anyone who may be hiring. The contacts that we are connected to can be referred to as the hidden job market. It's that simple. Many employers like to hire individuals who have been referred by people they know. It gives them a sense of comfort knowing that the referral comes from a reputable source. If you only knew five (5) people in this world and they knew five (5) people, and so on, then your access to contacts indirectly is very high. Accessing the potential information that exists in your network is critical to your success. Conducting a social network audit, as described in Job Search Ingredient #5, is the first thing you need to do in order to start tapping into the hidden job market.

If you stay true to the recipe, your chances of job search success will improve.

In your first couple of interviews, you will have to make an effort to move your agenda forward. At first, you will realize only after an interview that your agenda was not followed. However, eventually, following the approach in this book will become more automatic. You will start to see the Job Search Process, and the nature of the Hiring Cycle without further thought. It takes practice, but if you continue to implement these job search skills, they will become part of your routine, and, therefore, the time it will take to find a job will be dramatically decreased.

The job search itself is a challenging task. Keep in mind that you are going to have your good days and bad ones. This is a natural feeling and one that should be anticipated. The Job Search Board will provide you with the framework you need to understand what you've done in your job search and where you need to go. Use the Job Search Board as a tool for defining what you actually do during your job search. The structure of the Job Search Board will give you a sense of accomplishment and make you realize what you need to do differently. Whatever the case, you will now be able to follow a process that will help you find a job and provide you with immediate feedback.

The Job Search Never Ends

You've spent the last number of weeks looking for work. It's been gruelling; you have had to overcome rejection after rejection. However, even though you've accomplished your goal of employment, the hard work needs to continue. Now that you have found a job you need to continue to job search and keep your momentum moving forward. The job search is a natural extension of your career development; as you explore your career options, you need to continue to work on creating job opportunities. By this I mean you must continue to build your contact list, such that there is both the possibility for promotion within your new organization, as well as the generation of new job opportunities outside of it. It is important that you keep up this momentum in terms of looking for work by growing your network to include individuals that can help you achieve your goals. Although you have spent a period of time working hard finding a job and may think that the process is over, it's actually just begun if you were to look at it from a career perspective. If, for any reason, you leave this newly acquired position in the future, you need to keep in mind that in order to improve your chances of finding new work, you must continue to be identifying job opportunities. The continuous Job Search Process is one in which you expand your career horizons, by applying the concepts presented in this book.

Job Search Activity: (JSS: 4-1) The Continuous Job Search Process

The best way to find a job is when you are already employed; this is usually when it occurs. Your network automatically expands, and the ability to be connected to new job opportunities increases. The key is to remain active and aware in your job search and look at ways to build your career and move it in the direction you desire.

How to Keep Cooking

The key to keeping the job search going is by developing a career Action Plan that is in keeping with your desired goals. I highly recommend you sit down with a career counsellor and create a plan. Most people think that once they've acquired a job they no longer require the services of a career counsellor. This is a big mistake. It is at this stage that one needs to sit down with someone to develop a plan on how you are going to reach your career objectives. The reason you should do this at this stage of your career is that in most cases you will have access to new resources (i.e. people, training, experiences) that can help you move your goal forward. In order to maintain the momentum you have generated over the last number of weeks, you should create a career Action Plan that will keep your job search moving forward. The following exercise will help you develop a strategy.

Job Search Activity: (JSA: 4-2) Sample Career Action Questionnaire

Instructions: *Take a look at the following questions and answer them after you have landed a job. Whether you are just starting your career or have changed jobs, the career action questionnaire is important to your future success. Keep in mind that your answers to these questions will change throughout your tenure with the new organization.*

1. What is my ultimate career goal?

_____

_____

_____

_____

_____

2. How will my present position help me reach my career goal(s)?

_____

_____

_____

_____

3. Is there any individual in the organization that can assist me in meeting my career goal(s)? How?

_____

_____

4. Who, outside the organization, can help me achieve my career goal(s)?

_____

_____

_____

_____

5. What training can I participate in (with this organization), that will help me reach my career goal(s)?

_____

_____

_____

_____

6. What additional training/education can I acquire outside of my present organization that can help me reach my career goal(s)?

_____

_____

_____

_____

Some of the areas that you need to focus on during your continuous job search, include:

- Continue to make connections by joining associations and volunteering

- Keep your resume updated

- Be aware of changing labour market conditions

- Find a mentor

- Maintain an up-to-date career Action Plan

- Attend training and educational activities, which relate to your career goals

- Continue to assess your skills and abilities to ensure they are in keeping with your area of expertise

- Always look for new job opportunities (within your organization or outside)

Taking the Taste Test

The amazing thing about the process to which you have just been introduced is that you most likely have been using many of the skills described in this book already. What this book has provided you is the ability to organize your job search in a certain way so that you can easily recall the skills you require, for use as needed. The book has provided a framework for your job search that will allow you to identify areas of strength and weakness. Your goal is to continue with your strengths and reduce your weaknesses. However, you must first be aware of your weaknesses, and the process that is introduced here will allow you to do exactly that.

When you start to use your Job Search Board you will be amazingly surprised by the structure and purpose the Job Search Management Recipe provides. The Job Search Board will become your most important "utensil" and provides a readily available report on where you're at in the Job Search Process. The most important aspect of this unique recipe is that it will allow you to monitor your job lead opportunities and keep track of them throughout the Hiring Cycle.

A critical factor to success in your job search is how you will deal with the Job Search Forces introduced to you in Part One. The key here is to understand that your job search activity is directly related to your motivation and your motivation is directly related to your ability to have a realistic outlook in what you are doing. If one of these forces is adversely affected, your entire job search may be jeopardized. Remember the forces when you feel that you have reached the bottom and ask yourself the following questions:

- What am I doing on a daily basis to look for work?
- How long do I actually spend doing job search activities?
- How have I been identifying job opportunities?
- What is the movement of my Job Search Board?
- How am I matching my skills to the opportunities I'm identifying?
- How many new people have I met in the last couple of weeks?
- How many people actually know that I am looking for work?

I'm sure you can think of a number of other questions. The important factor here is to know that you are likely to feel discouraged at times throughout your job search. The reality is that you will receive a lot of rejection during this process and you have to be aware of that. When you submit a resume or fill out an application, remember to determine the job search odds. This will prepare you for whatever happens.

As previously noted, the Job Search Board will provide you with the structure you require to succeed. Collecting your job search numbers will provide you with a visual indicator of precisely what you are doing and what you can do better -- a numerical benchmark of what you have to do on a daily basis. Finding your ideal number will take some time. If you find that you have been averaging five (5) job leads a day, use that number as a bench mark. When you have identified five (5) job opportunities for the day, you're done. Go on to something else, do something completely different. By doing this you have put some parameters around your job search, and won't feel guilty when you're doing activities unrelated to your job search. By the same token, you now know that you will not have completed your job search for a given day until you have identified five (5) job leads and applied to them. Everyone will have a different number of job leads. Take some time to determine what yours is and use that number as a measurement for activity.

Whatever you do during your job search, the key is to remember that there is a timeframe associated with looking for work. Every employer has a general timeframe in mind, by the end of which they will need to have secured a new employee. If you're not working within that timeframe, the likelihood of getting the job drastically decreases. How do you know what the timeframe is? The only way to determine the timeframe is by contacting employers on a regular basis. As long as you realize that Hiring Cycles are happening every day, you will be more likely to be knocking on employers' doors. The old adage of "Being at the right place at the right time" certainly holds true in the Job Search Process, and, therefore, the only way you can be at the right place at the right time is by doing it everyday.

Managing your Job Search Online

You might want to consider moving your job search online by going to www.snagpad.com. This website has been created to help you manage every aspect of your job search in one central online location. The 'Job Search Board' allows you monitor each job opportunity you identify. Snag Pad can tie into your Facebook or LinkedIn contacts, provides process-oriented strategies, serves as a virtual job coach and administers challenges to guide desired behaviour and actions needed to find the right job faster. Job opportunities "snagged" from any originating source, convert to Job Cards™, which you can manage and share via your "Pad". Additionally, you can start your very own "employment network" to increase your exposure to the hidden job market.

Job Search Activity: (JSS: 4-3) Creating an account on SnagPad.com

Go to http://www.snagpad.com and set up an account for free. By using snagpad.com as your job search management system you will be able to centralize all of your job search activity online.

Final Thoughts on the Job Search Recipe

Now that you have been exposed to the Job Search Recipe, you need to practice it by putting it all together. Make sure you have the proper "utensils", and your chances of being successful will dramatically increase. Like any great dish, it takes time to learn the details of preparing it. The same holds true for conducting a job search. The more you get out and practice the techniques, the better you'll get at finding a job. Learn from your challenges and build strategies for overcoming them. **If you stay true to the recipe, your chances of job search success will improve.**

APPENDIX - TASTE TEST ANSWERS

Taste Test: **(TT: 1-1) The Realistic Job Search - Understanding the job search odds**

Sample Job Opportunities

Job Opportunity #1 – Newspaper Ad

Customer Service Representative

Working within our commodity trading department, and emphasizing excellent customer service, this position is responsible for processing sales orders and customer inquiries in a timely, efficient, and proactive manner. The successful candidate will: enter sales contracts; schedule shipments; answer customer inquiries regarding invoice/contract details, load-order status, contract position, and unpriced product; generate invoices; prepare sales reports; and ensure credit and inventory issues are addressed.

Qualified candidates will possess a post-secondary business diploma and have two years experience in a sales-related environment, with a demonstrated aptitude for superior customer service. Proficiency with PC applications, such as Word and Excel, is required, and experience with SAP would be an asset.

Qualified candidates should forward a resume no later than September 17, 2006.

Beth Armstrong
XYZ Company
3456 Somewhere Street
beth.armstrong@xyzcompany.com

- The odds are low due to the fact that it comes from a newspaper.

- There is no referral

- The job seeker has some of the qualifications, but no direct experience.

- The job seeker has some of the skills required.

- The job seeker has no experience with SAP.

Job Opportunity #2 – Verbal Job Lead

Job Opportunity for an Inside Sales Representative, from a friend of a friend

The individual's close friend advises them to call another friend to find out more about an opportunity for an Inside Sales Representative position. They call this friend and, after introductions, she begins to talk about a position within her organization as an Inside Sales Representative. She is the assistant to the sales manager, who will be the individual conducting the interviews. The position requires: some experience in sales; computer skills; and access to a vehicle. The assistant provides the individual with the manager's name and phone number, and suggests that they use her name when they submit their resume.

- Chances are very good, as there is a direct referral.

- It's an entry-level position, so the odds are that it will not require extensive experience.

- The job seeker has some related experience from the call centre.

- The job seeker has some of the skills the position requires.

Job Opportunity #3 – Cold Call

Cold call at a Telecommunications company – Human Resource Department

The individual calls up a large telecommunications company and is directed to their Human Resources department. They ask if the company is hiring for any of their sales departments. The HR person provides them with an anonymous email where they can submit their resume for consideration for openings. However, they are unsure of any specific position, "at this time", which they will need to fill in the sales department.

- Chances may be low.

- No specific referral source.

- No information that they may be even hiring.

- Didn't get the name of the sales manager.

Taste Test: (TT: 1-2) Job Search Forces and Control

1. Activity, Motivation, and a having a Realistic outlook.

2. Managing a realistic outlook and maintaining high level of job search activity.

3. All.

4. They are low because: Many people will apply; you may not be able to address your cover letter to a specific person; it is not a referral source; or there is limited information on opportunity.

5. True.

Taste Test: (TT: 2-1) Job Search Numbers

1. Job Opportunities (JO), Applied (A) and Set Interviews (SI).

2. So the job seeker has an idea of what her job search activity is and how she can improve her approach. The job search numbers provide a benchmark for activity and assists in identifying specific challenges associated with the job search.

3. The benefits of a "targeted approach" to your job search include: having a customized approach to the job opportunity; that it becomes directed to a particular individual; that it increases your job search odds; and that it highlights the job seeker's skills and abilities, as per a given employer's needs.

4. The benefits include: less energy spent on opportunities, ability to maintain a high level of activity and increased chances of getting interviews. The challenges include: it not being addressed to anyone specifically, it not being targeted, it yielding lower quality opportunities.

5. How long has this person been looking? What happened to the other eight (8) opportunities that weren't applied to? Why is there only one (1) set interview? What are the specific opportunities to which the individual is applying?

Taste Test: (TT: 2-2) The What, Who, Where, When and Why

1. It's more efficient to focus on what you are doing during your job search than what you need. Whenever you can describe what you're doing, you can find ways of doing it better.
2. A response in your own words is required here.
3. A response in your own words is required here.

Taste Test: (TT: 2-3) The Hiring Cycle

1. As early as possible or prior to the application deadline.
2. a, b, c, d.
3. A response in your own words is required here.

Taste Test: (TT: 2-4) The Next Step

1. The "next step" is different in following up in that it is a proactive approach to generating a next step in the Job Search Process. If you don't know what is going to happen from one stage to another, you have not generated a next step. Following-up simply refers to checking the status of your application, or how you did after an interview.

2. a, c, d.

3. The main items are in identifying: the right person, the right process, the right timeframe, the right position, and the right salary.

4. The biggest impact will be on your motivation. Not knowing what will occur next in the Job Search Process will deeply affect a job seeker's ability to remain focused, which is the reason behind the importance of identifying the next step.

Taste Test: (TT: 2-5) Identifying Job Opportunities

1. You can go to: your network, religious leaders, elected government officials, teachers, newspaper, Internet, volunteering, associations, breakfast clubs, directories, cold calls (i.e. to employers directly), and/or referrals.

2. d.

3. True.

4. True

5. True

6. A response in your own words is required here

Taste Test: (TT: 2-6) Applying to the job opportunity

1. You can determine which one by looking at the job search odds, and whether you, as the job seeker, have a likelihood of getting the job, based on your skills and abilities matching the opportunity. If there is not a good match, the generic resume should be submitted. If there is a close match, the targeted resume should be submitted.

2. a, b, c.

3. One page.

4. A response in your own words is required here.

5. A response in your own words is required here.

Taste Test: (TT: 2-7) Setting the interview

1. c.

2. A response in your own words is required here.

3. A response in your own words is required here.

4. d.

Taste Test: (TT: 2-8) Going to the interview

1.   A response in your own words is required here.

2.   Some good signs are: The interviewer is taking a lot of notes; following to your answers; starts to say things like, *"When you start, you will be provided with..."*; and the interviewer provides you with a definite next step.

3.   The information to collect includes: to determine who the position reports to, knowledge of their Hiring Cycle, to identify the timeframe for when the position begins, to know the hiring process, and to identify the salary.

Taste Test: (TT: 2-9) Receiving the job offer

1.   "In terms of salary, how does your organization compare to the competition?"

2.   A response in your own words is required here.

Taste Test: (TT: 2-10) Let the job begin

1.   a, c ,d

2.   Things to consider when you first start your new job include: get some rest; dress for success; arrive early; make sure people know who you are; assess the corporate culture; identify opinion leaders; identify key players; find out what your new employer expects of you; seek help from co-workers; remain neutral, be flexible.

3.   True.

4.   A response in your own words is required here.

About the Author

Dr. Hatala brings more than 15 years of experience in the community, the public and private sectors. He has worked in such diverse capacities as: employment counselor; job developer, small business consultant, training and development manager, Director of Human Resources and university professor.

Dr. Hatala is presently an Assistant Professor at the Rochester Institute of Technology in the Human Resource Development Program, a Senior Research Fellow at the University of Ottawa and an Adjunct Professor at Louisiana State University in the School of Human Resource Education and Workforce Development. He is also the founder of the social capital development firm Flowork International.

His research has focused on the transition towards re-employment, job search, human resource development, social capital, career and organizational development. John-Paul was awarded the Elwood F. Holton III Research Excellence Award for his paper entitled "Social Network Analysis: A New Methodology for Human Resource Development".

He is the author of over 100 publications examining the impact of social capital on individuals and organizations. Dr. Hatala has made numerous presentations at a number of conferences and venues, including: the National Consultation on Career Development and Worforce Learning; Canadian Education and Research Institute for Counseling; American Society for Training and Development; and the Academy of Human Resource Development Conference.

To date, Dr. Hatala has developed a number of innovative systems and assessment tools including: Networking Management System (includes the network analysis and network monitoring system); Strategic Job Search Management System (includes a monitoring system for labor market re-entry); and a series of assessments, including the Social Exploration Learning Form (SELF), BEST for adults and BEST for youth (Barriers to Entrepreneurship Success Tools).

Born in Canada, Dr. Hatala received his PhD from the University of Toronto in 2003. He is married with three childern, and resides in Burlington, Ontario, Canada.

John-Paul encourages you to connect with him.

Online Coordinates:

Twitter – @jphatala

LinkedIn – John-Paul Hatala

Website – http://www.flowork.com

Email – jphatala@flowork.com

Made in the USA
Charleston, SC
24 December 2012